"Will Leverette was fortunate enough to have grown up in the North Carolina summer camp community where paddling history was being made. Reading his stories reminds me of listening to someone, while sitting around a campfire, after a paddling trip, telling tales of the day's adventures. He will bring back fond memories of past canoe trips to you as he has for me. Not only does Will present the history of canoeing and canoes, he puts real life into the history."

—Bob Benner, *author*
Carolina White Water, A Paddler's Guide
to The Western Carolinas, *thirteen editions*

"This is a fascinating memoir by a man who grew up as the grandson of the legendary Frank 'Chief' Bell at summer camps which were owned and operated by members of the Bell family in the mountains of Western North Carolina. The thousands of adults who in their youth attended the camps where Leverette grew up or other camps in the area will be reminded of the many adventures of those formative years, and some may be inspired to pick up a paddle once again."

—Payson Kennedy
*Founder and president of the
Nantahala Outdoor Center*

"This book brought me back to the memory of my first couple of strokes in a kayak! Will Leverette is a great storyteller, and he manages to explore the Southeast's rich paddling history while reminding us all of our humble beginnings with moving water. This book has been a long time coming."

—Chris Gragtmans
three-time Canadian Freestyle Team Member; Canadian Junior Champion 2002, 2003; Green River Narrows Race Ironman Winner, 2005

"Will captures the essence, elegance, simplicity and absurdity of those early whitewater paddling years in Western North Carolina where we paddled so many rivers with so little equipment."

—Bunny Johns
Past president of the Nantahala Outdoor Center

Frank Bell, Ray Eaton, Perry Patterson, Alice Gordon Chalmers, Bunny Johns and Hugh Caldwell on the banks of the Chattooga River, 1960s.

A History of
WHITEWATER
PADDLING
in Western North Carolina

Water Wise

Will Leverette

Charleston   London

THE
History
PRESS

Published by The History Press
Charleston, SC 29403
www.historypress.net

Copyright © 2008 by Will Leverette
All rights reserved

Cover design by Natasha Momberger.

All images are courtesy of the author.

First published 2008

Manufactured in the United Kingdom

ISBN 978.1.59629.435.6

Library of Congress Cataloging-in-Publication Data
Leverette, Will.
A history of whitewater paddling in western North Carolina: water
wise / Will Leverette.
p. cm.
Includes bibliographical references and index.
ISBN 978-1-59629-435-6 (alk. paper)
1. White-water canoeing--North Carolina--Guidebooks. 2. Canoes
and canoeing--North Carolina--Guidebooks. 3. North Carolina--
Guidebooks. I. Leverette, Will. II. Title.
GV776.N74W56 2008
797.12209756--dc22
                                    2008018156

*This history of whitewater paddling in
Western North Carolina is dedicated to:
my father Bill Leverette for teaching me the value of
history and writing;*

*To my mother Pat (Bell) Leverette for teaching me
how to live;*

To Ray Eaton for teaching me how to paddle.

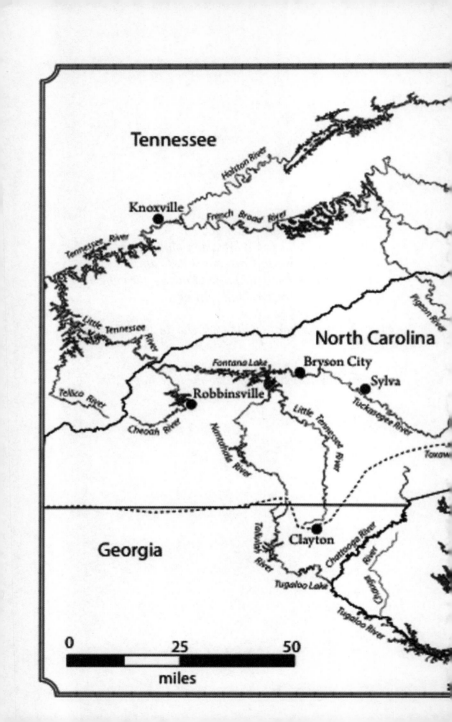

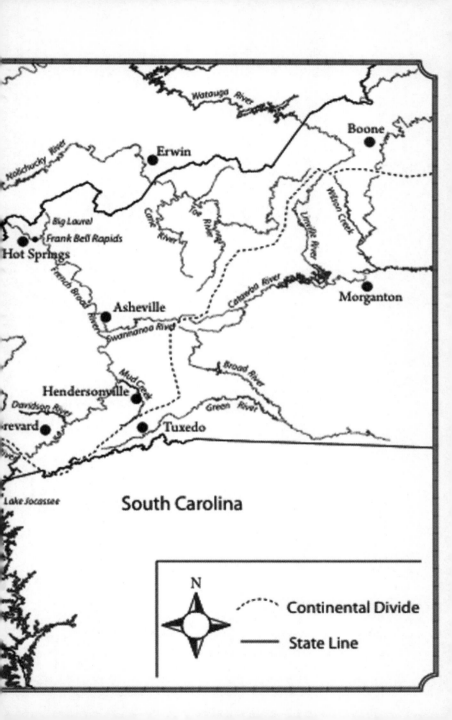

CONTENTS

ACKNOWLEDGEMENTS

Community is one of those qualities that is missing from today's modern world. This book has been the result of a community effort. Many people contributed their time and talent.

First of all I would like to thank all the people whom I interviewed and who gave me many of the stories found here.

Pat Leverette, my mom, who has passed into that great river in the sky: thanks for who I am and for teaching me about forgiveness and love.

Bob Benner, Bunny Johns, Payson Kennedy, Frank Bell Jr., Perry Patterson, Alice Gordon Chalmers, Terrill Garrard, David William, Fritz Orr Jr. and Fritz Orr III: thank you. I love you all, I salute your past and present. If I could ever paddle with any of you again, I'll die a happy man.

Laura Hermann and Arlin Geyer helped scan and improve my dusty old photographs and solve my computer problems.

Camps High Rocks, Mondamin and Green Cove all contributed photographs, as did Calla Bell and Fritz Orr III.

Acknowledgements

Ray Russell and the Barnes and Noble Writers' Workshop edited and gave me great lessons in writing.

Kerri Saum, my transcriptionist and inspiration: without you this project would have stayed on the back burner and would never have happened.

Molly McMillan and Michael Hopping, real writers, were my best editors.

Sam Fowlkes helped me with the interviews when I needed it the most.

The Dixie Division of the American Canoe Association gave me timely seed money.

Kent Ford inspired me when I needed a kick in the pants.

My sister Ann gave me a laptop when I needed one and provided excellent editing. I need lots of editing.

My father Bill Leverette, who died in 2002, inspired my love of history and writing. Dad, I did it! It's about Mom's crazy family, but I did it.

To the thousands of students I have had the pleasure of teaching for these past thirty-four years, thank you. I learned more than I taught.

Rick Lindsey in Salt Lake City, thank you for giving me meaningful work related to my love for rivers.

To all the rivers in the western hemisphere I have had the privilege and honor of loving passionately: I owe it all to you.

Thanks go to Warren Wilson College for giving me the exalted position as paddling mentor in residence (aka, designated old fart) so I could continue to tell college students about the appropriate uses of speed in sex, I mean paddling.

David Moore and Andrea Glenn put together the map of Western North Carolina rivers.

Thanks also to Susan Kask, who straightened out my computer confusion when I was ready to scream.

Thanks too have to go to Lee Handford, Laura All and The History Press for believing in my vision and me.

Jack McCallie believed in me from the start and was my paddling partner growing up at camp. Brother, I will never forget you.

Thanks everybody, I love you.

INTRODUCTION

Paddling has saved my life. Around 1989 I was diagnosed with multiple sclerosis while living in Salt Lake City, Utah. While I had grown up and been raised as a paddler, later in life I had discovered the joys of rock climbing and skiing and had virtually dropped paddling as an obsession. When I could no longer climb and ski I thought my life was over. For my first five years of living with the disease I experienced a number of what the doctors called remissions or exacerbations. I'd get very sick and be unable to drive a car, hold a fork or work, much less ski and climb. I even went blind in my left eye. Every time I would go down hard, one of my parents would fly out to Salt Lake from North Carolina to nurse me back to health. After a few years of this, I began to feel really guilty, as my dad could handle the trips out to Utah but my poor mom was struggling. She had rheumatoid arthritis and Parkinson's disease and the trips were taking an obvious toll.

I decided that my life was over because I couldn't ski and climb anymore, and that the thing to do was going to be to kill myself. I thought that it would be best to do it in North Carolina because, in my typical codependent thinking, it would be easier on my parents if I did it at home. During an exacerbation that my dad had flown out to deal with, I decided to come with him back to Asheville to do the dirty deed. While back on my old turf, I shared my plan with an old friend, Pat Patton, who was a chiropractor and someone I had worked with at Camp Woodson, a camping program for juvenile delinquents with the North Carolina Department of Youth Corrections.

Pat said, "Hold the phone. I've learned some things and I'd like to try them out on you."

I said, "Okay," and began the strictest dietary regime you have ever heard of. About the same time someone shared with me a Chinese proverb that basically states that the single greatest challenge (read that as opportunity) that we as humans face in our lifetime is to take our biggest weakness and turn it into our biggest strength.

Whoa! That hit me like a ton of bricks and I decided that my greatest weakness (MS) was somehow going to become my greatest strength. I quit hating MS. I quit having a perpetual pity party for myself and I got on with my life. I might not be able to ski and climb anymore, but I figured I could still paddle. My boss in Salt Lake, Rick Lindsey, had given me an inflatable kayak, commonly known as a duck, and I began to search out some of my old paddling family and friends. Rick had allowed me to continue my work back in North Carolina with the liability insurance program as a recreation and safety specialist and risk manager. I had work. I had friends and family and I had paddling, my old friend. I found a cute little house with very little effort and settled in for the long, happy haul.

"My greatest weakness is my greatest strength."

Who'd a thunk it? Getting MS gave me the opportunity to take a look at myself in ways that I probably wouldn't have otherwise. I've learned more about what's important in life than I might have. I've gained a very real appreciation for my family and friends, warts and all, and for each sunrise.

In very little time I was paddling class-four rivers again and actually went on to paddle some of the most proud and difficult rivers of my life. Inflatable kayaks gave me the opportunity to be on the river again and I have Brad McCallister of Vista Kayaks to thank for designing and building high-performance inflatable boats. I also began to think that someone needed to write down a lot of this paddling history stuff. I asked my grandmother Cala if I could go though her dark room and "borrow" any paddling-related photos I could find. Cala had been the camp photographer for many years and she had a dark room in her and Frank Bell's house. Thank god I did that, as the house has since burned and most of the photos in this book would have been badly smoke damaged.

Although I have taken paddling some places I've never been before, I really don't need difficulty to fill my heart anymore. I've paddled the lower Green a thousand times, and I'll die a happy man if I can paddle it a hundred more times. There is nothing I like more than taking some newbies down the river and seeing the joy on their faces as they surf Sunshine Ledge for the first time. That's a good day for me.

I recently bought a recumbent tricycle and between paddling, biking and swimming have managed to keep myself fairly fit. My neurologist says I am his healthiest MS patient, and I have a Chinese proverb to thank. Suicide didn't really sit that well with me. It didn't seem like me and the choice to live seemed better. I have challenges, but I couldn't be happier. Warren Wilson College has given me the opportunity to continue to teach paddling, my greatest lifelong passion, and Rick Lindsey, my boss, has continued to give me meaningful work. My circle of friends and family continues to grow. I'm the happiest big camper you'll ever know.

This history, therefore, is a history of my life, the people I have had the privilege to know and the rivers and experiences I have been blessed to be a part of. Our history is an amazing thing, partly because of its ability

19

to teach us lessons from the mistakes of others, partly because of its wonderful ability to weave stories, entertain and inspire imagination but mostly because it's ours. My father was a history professor at Furman University for thirty years and I never got it. I think I do now, and I know that he would be so proud of the fact that I have undertaken to write this history.

Therefore, the following information is to be read and enjoyed as if you are sitting around a campfire listening to one of the camp elders spin tales of yesteryear the night before the next day's big river trip. We will probably never know the full truth but we can be inspired by the tales of women and men who were there many years ago, pioneering the way unself-consciously and unaware of the importance and significance of what they were doing. This is a proud and interesting history that is filled with colorful characters doing very amazing things, and I can only hope that I am able to tell some of the story with accuracy, a lot of humility and some humor. Kind of like the way that they lived their lives. So this is how so it was, I think...

HOW SO IT WAS

There is nothing—absolutely nothing—half so much worth doing as simply messing about in boats.
—*Kenneth Grahame,* The Wind in the Willows, *1908*

I had been wired and plumbed from a very early age to become a paddler. Ray Eaton gave me my first paddle when I was three, which is about the age I started going to camp with my mother, who ran the paddling program. By seven I was on my first river trip. Al Moore, a camp counselor at my grandfather's Camp Mondamin, once claims he caught my parents in, shall we say, an amorous situation in a canoe on Lake Pontchartrain when they were teaching and working at New Orleans Country Day School. I was born about nine months later and so the legend became that I was conceived in a canoe.

Apparently my first word was "water," and I remember well my first experience floating a rapid. When my sister Ann and I were little, our parents would take us to the Green River near Saluda, North Carolina, to camp out on the beach at the bottom of Little Corky Rapid. Mom had always been a big customer of the Army Surplus store in Greenville,

South Carolina. We slept on green Army Surplus air mattresses inside a giant canvas family tent.

During the day our parents would take us to the river to run the rapids on those air mattresses. Dad would gingerly walk out into the river above a little rapid with my sister or me and position us prone onto the raft, and then let us go. Mom would be waiting in the pool at the bottom, where she would catch us. I'm sure that we were just like most kids anytime you do something fun with them, and our response was, "Do it again! Do it again!" Of course we were not wearing life jackets, and that is the way it was for me for many years growing up at camp and running rivers.

The maintenance man, Dee Stanley, at Camp High Rocks in Cedar Mountain, North Carolina, where I grew up and learned to paddle, used to always say, "Now, I don't know how so it is, but from what I hear…" Dee didn't always speak the Queen's English, but he spoke with more mountain common sense and wisdom than most. My time with Dee began each day at 6:00 a.m., when I would walk down to the barn to muck stalls. As I crossed the road and fields next to the barn, swallows would dive bomb me and announce my arrival to the horses.

Dee would pull the manure spreader around to the stalls with the Massey Ferguson and my Aunt Jane would join us with a smile. We would take up our weapons, nine-tined pitchforks, and very gently lift each little round horse turd off the straw that lies on the bottom of the stall and pitch it into the manure spreader to be taken out to the pastures. Jane and Dee were gently insistent that the masterful stall mucker could slide the tines of the pitchfork just under each little morsel so carefully that no straw would be wasted.

As I learned precise placement of the pitchfork, I was also learning precise paddle placement at the slalom gates on the lake at camp. By the time I was a teenager, a cove on the lake had been strung with slalom gate poles hanging from wires between trees on shore, and there we practiced the fine art of boat control. The gates were hung in pairs and the goal was to negotiate a prescribed course through them without touching the poles. Long before whitewater racing had introduced slalom paddling, my mother got the idea that putting something on the lake at the camp as obstacles for the kids to paddle around was a good teaching tool.

One winter before the gates were hung, she bought a bunch of duck decoys to be used for hunting. We spent the winter painstakingly painting ducks onto the decoys with patterns we got out of a bird book. As the dense papier-mâché that the decoys were made of soaked up water they became heavy, and the freeze and thaw of the lake each year took their toll. We used that slalom course for years, until the ducks eventually all sank. Years later the dam on the lake went out and there, on the bottom of the lake, were the decoys. Several people asked what all those decoys were doing there, as no one had ever hunted at camp, but I remember them fondly.

Will Leverette practicing on the slalom gates at the Camp High Rocks Lake in a wood and fiberglass canoe, 1978.

The pitchfork and the paddle were the same in my adolescent mind. Both had to be wielded with care and accuracy to achieve the desired results. After my shift at the barn I would run up to the dining hall where, after washing the pots from breakfast, my real day would truly begin. I would hurry down to the canoe dock and begin to teach the rudiments of boat control necessary to successfully negotiate a rapid to whomever wanted to learn, just as my elders had done for me.

By the time I was sixteen, my skills on the dock became more valuable than my skills in the barn and in the kitchen, and they put me on the dock full time. I was in heaven and decided at that young age that I was going to make a living teaching paddling, which I'm still doing. Eventually my skills with a paddle led to numerous raft guiding and paddling jobs, followed by a career as a risk manager with the largest liability insurer for outfitters and guides in the country, the Worldwide Outfitter and Guide Association.

Dee must have thought we were a bit crazy as he drove numerous shuttles for us while we ran rivers all over the western end of the state. A shuttle is necessary because boaters need a vehicle at the bottom, or take-out, at the end of the trip. Dee performed a valuable function, as he often was the "shuttle bunny" for camp trips.

As I sit down to write some of my family's history, I pause to figure out how to resolve what I see as an inherent conundrum in the whole process. How do you tell the stories of some events that took place forty years ago, events that I believe to be factual, but about which no one will ever know as indisputable? After all, we weren't there.

Given that I am already perceived to be something of an expert—in part due to my family history, in part due to my experience as a paddler and in part due to the fact that I have become an old-timer, the designated "old fart" just like the Ramone (Ray) Eatons and Bill Doswells of camp— I decided to write some of these legends down before I'm dead too.

It seems like only yesterday when I would see Ray paddling quietly through the North Carolina mountain mist on the High Rocks Lake at sunset. Now it's up to me to paddle quietly through the mist and say something intelligent to the kids. Sometimes that's more of a challenge than I'm willing to admit.

Perhaps because I knew all these people, perhaps because I've heard too many stories or perhaps because I want to believe them, I'm choosing to mostly believe them and I suggest you do too. The information presented here is presented as fact. This is a collection of camp stories that I have grown up with regarding an extraordinary group of people whom I loved devotedly. So, I don't know how so it was but...

In 1920, Frank Bell, my grandfather, known to everyone as Chief, moved to Texas to start a summer camp. While there, he and his wife Hannah had their first of three daughters, also Hannah but later known as Pat. That camp failed, but Chief went on to build Camp Mondamin for boys and Camp Green Cove for girls on Lake Summit in Tuxedo, North Carolina. To this day these camps have the finest camp paddling programs for kids in the country. Mom was the first director of Camp Green Cove, which was held on the site of Camp Rockbrook in Brevard, North Carolina. Mom later decided that being a camp director was a little too close to the life she had grown up with and became a school counselor instead. Chief had inherited the property on Lake Summit that was to become Camps Mondamin and Green Cove from his father, Oscar Bell, who had built the town in the early 1900s, along with the Green River Mill that manufactured textiles. When he built the town someone asked him what he wanted to name it. Supposedly he pondered for a moment and said, "I don't know. Let's dress it up and call it Tuxedo."

Chief had gone to a camp as a child in Transylvania County called the French Broad River Camp, and the experience left quite an impression on him. Paddling the pastoral French Broad near Brevard as a young boy, Chief

Sail canoes on Lake Summit, Camp Mondamin, 1930s.

had no way of knowing that in 1923 the biggest rapid on the run would be named for him because he destroyed a wooden canoe while paddling it.

From the start Chief wanted his camps to be all about wilderness skills and appreciation. Young boys and girls were taught about outdoor adventure–based activities such as rock climbing, whitewater canoeing, backpacking and horse packing.

Chief was an interesting man to tolerate. Charismatic and visionary as a camp director, he was intimidating and larger than life as my grandfather. He was a "pulled up by the bootstraps" kind of man and did not tolerate any signs of weakness in other men. He competed with every man he ever met, and flirted with every woman he ever met. One of the pillars of camp philosophy was a disdain for organized competition. Camp was to be all about being the best a person could be, not about beating the other guy. This apparent conflict in Chief's approach toward competition was one of his personality quirks.

One of the most interesting things about Chief was what I saw as a strong belief in self-reliance. Yet I knew

Chief getting a drink of water on the edge of the Chattooga River at the bottom of the Narrows, 1960s.

that when the big man went on a camping trip he always brought his cook, a black man named Rudolf. A cook on a camping trip! He had even taken Rudolf with him when he went to college at the University of North Carolina, where he played football and drove a Stutz Bearcat, the sports car of the day. When I was a child, going to Chief's house for Thanksgiving and Christmas dinner was a joyful time with our big family, and the food was amazing. Rudolf, oftentimes drunk, and Queen, Chief's other black servant (who also worked on Christmas Day), would come out of the kitchen and serve us the most magnificent feasts imaginable. It wasn't until I became a teenager and began to figure a few things out and my mom explained some things to me that I started to wonder about this relationship that Chief had with his "servants." Regardless, the man was a huge inspiration to me and this symbol of the great, independent camp director and whitewater pioneer was pivotal in my growth.

Beginning in the 1960s, Mondamin staff and later campers went on to pioneer a lot of Southern classics. Steve Longnecker, a climbing counselor, climbed the Nose on Looking Glass for the first time and in 1964 my mom and Ray Eaton took a group of Camp High Rocks girls down section three of the Chattooga, the earliest guided descents of that river by a family camp group.

Mondamin quickly became the premier summer camping program in the country for developing whitewater paddling skills. Mondamin has put twelve people on the U.S. Whitewater Paddling Team through the years. None of this would have happened if it were not for the influence of one extraordinary man, Raymon Eaton, known to everyone at that time as Ray.

Before 1972, the only people we saw on the rivers of Western North Carolina were affiliated with one of four summer camps: Merrie Woode of Cashiers; Mondamin or Green Cove of Tuxedo; or High Rocks of Cedar Mountain, all located in the beautiful mountains of Western North Carolina. Ray spent a great deal of time at each of these camps and in the process gave inspiration to a lot of some of the next thirty years' most influential paddlers, like Bunny Johns, Gordon Grant and Lecky Haller. Ray paddled with such grace and ease that whole generations of paddlers have spent their lives trying to paddle like him. He could paddle the entire Nantahala Falls and never take a single stroke. It was poetry.

Ray gave me my first paddle when I was three years old and later heavily influenced the directions my life would take. Ray was at Camp High Rocks during my very formative adolescent years and inspired me to work with anyone I could get to listen to me regarding whitewater boating. It wasn't hard to get an audience and before I knew it, I had parlayed my avocation into a vocation and I was fifty years old. Ray used to tell me about a concept that I thought made a lot of sense. A person who possessed quiet competence in a wide variety of water-related skills such as paddling, swimming, sailing, water-skiing, snorkeling and diving was someone who was "water wise." It took a lot of experience to add up to that designation. Being "water wise" was something that

Ray Eaton in a Grumman canoe at Nantahala Falls, Nantahala River, 1950s.

carried a great deal of weight and respect. There really weren't that many people around who even deserved the moniker. I decided that I should aspire to that status myself, and so I began a lifelong pursuit of all skills and experiences that had anything to do with water. I sought, later in life, to be competent in all types of craft on all types of moving water: canoes, kayaks, C-1s and C-2s, paddle rafts and oar rigs. I wanted it all.

Ray brought one of those hollow, wooden surfboards from Hawaii to camp. When motorboats first began to appear on Lake Summit, he got the cockeyed notion that he could stand on the board and be towed behind the boat. That became the first time anyone water-skied on Lake Summit and one of the first times anyone water-skied anywhere. That's the kind of a guy Ray was, and he was a great example of what it meant to be "water wise."

29

I will never forget my first real whitewater paddling experience, at age seven on the Davidson River near Brevard, North Carolina. I had been fussing around in canoes on the lake at High Rocks, where my mother ran the paddling program for the girls' camp session, not really getting what all the hubbub was about, when I made my first river trip. In those days we got enough rain to raise the little Davidson to a level that was a great run for first-timers.

I had some little camper girl as my partner and we put in at the pool right by the old English Chapel. The first rapid, if you can call it that, was a small ripple of a thing right at the outflow of the pool. We proceeded one boat at a time, partly to allow my mother the opportunity to give directions and encouragement to anyone who needed it and partly to keep everyone from piling up on one another as we would get stuck on the shallow river bottom. My partner and I entered the riffle and very quickly had to negotiate a small right turn at the bottom of the shoal. There was a little but very obvious rock to the left of the current near the bottom. As we approached the bend right above this rock, I could see that the current was going to take me, in the stern, right into it. Without instructions or help from my wading mother, I reached out to the right with a draw stroke to keep my end of the boat from hitting the obstruction. I was ecstatic and overjoyed at my success. For the first time in my life I got what all this foolishness was all about. I really thought that this was me. I liked this stuff, wanted more and began a river career that proved to be the most important thing that ever happened to me.

For the next two years, as I continued to grow and get stronger, I made many Davidson River trips. We would swamp canoes and try to hold onto them broadside in the current to simulate what to do with a swamped boat and feel the power of the current. If a rapid was too shallow, and many of them were, we would get out of our boats and stack rocks to enhance, or even create rapids. I remember my years on the mighty Davidson very fondly and still can't drive up the road along that river without being flooded with a kaleidoscope of great memories.

The Davidson is known for being the home of the infamous hellbender, an aquatic salamander that looks ferocious and like something out of a *Star Wars* movie. Hellbenders still exist in the Davidson and are a testament to that watershed's cleanliness and desirability as a trout stream. Also known as "snout otters" or "devil dogs," they

Camp Mondamin counselors in a wood and canvas canoe, high kneel, at Bridge Rapid on the Lower Green River, 1930s.

31

are terrifying to see and reach up to two and a half feet in length. They will bite only if provoked.

By the time I turned nine and could graduate from girls' camp to boys' camp, I was big and strong enough to step it up to the lower Green River. The lower Green had some real rapids and a couple of waves to play on. I was in heaven and proceeded rapidly through the progression of rivers that the camp used. I even developed quite a taste for the famous Green River sandwich, which consisted of pineapple and cheese.

I have learned a lot from paddling. At the tender age of twelve, I made the Nantahala River trip with camp. I had what I considered to be a very successful trip. Later that same summer, I made the Chattooga River trip. My paddling partner was a camper named Michael Wrentraub from Louisiana. While Michael had been sleeping on the ground at McGee Springs in the Smokies during a hike, a bear had bitten him right through his ankle. He and I did very well on the Nantahala, but the Chattooga is a whole other kettle of fish that requires a lot more boat control that apparently we didn't have. We paddled so poorly that Michael took numerous swims with his bandaged ankle and the counselors broke us up and put us each in a counselor's boat. I considered this to be the ultimate humility and upon returning to camp informed Bill Doswell, the director of the paddling program, that I felt good about having "conquered" the Nantahala but that the Chattooga had kicked my tail and I was miserable as a result. To my great surprise, he laughed.

He said, "You can never conquer a river. If you try to it will always kick your butt. What you want to do is find that place where you learn to go with the flow. Use the current to accomplish your goals, cooperate with the river, love its beauty and be thankful at the end of the day that the river let you descend it."

I felt like the biggest idiot in the world and learned a very valuable lesson that I have applied to the rest of my life. You can never "conquer" a river, a mountain, your fear or the backcountry. There's a better, more fulfilling way. I became the ultimate pacifist, someone in search of so much more than ego satisfaction in my journeys in the woods. This was a lesson that has influenced and guided me.

You'd think I would have learned a lot of these lessons from my mother, because she was remarkable. Not only did she pioneer the Nantahala in 1945 and take the first groups from camp down section three of the Chattooga in 1964, she was also an accomplished artist, child psychologist, carpenter and amazing mom. She had, in the early 1950s, chosen to go to New York City from Tuxedo, North Carolina, to study art at New York University. How many women who grow up in a backwater town like Tuxedo—where she went to grammar school in a one-room schoolhouse where her mother taught—choose to go to college in New York City? She did the finish carpentry work on the houses we lived in growing up and took my sister Ann and I and my river-clueless, college professor dad on camping and paddling trips to the Green River and the Everglades in her spare time. Mom was a liberated woman long before the concept became hip. She used her passion in art to become an accomplished potter, silversmith, rock mason and leather worker. Her carpentry skills were legendary and were nothing short of artwork itself.

I take great pride in the fact that I taught her, years later, how to surf a wave, something that had never occurred to the early pioneers of whitewater paddling. She took right to it and did a masterful job.

Mom, Ray, Chief and a handful of counselors drove out to California in 1949 or 1950 to paddle the Eel River. Ray borrowed wooden canoes from the Red Cross in California and they had a memorable trip and only smashed the end of one boat. I have a picture of my Mom crouching on the banks of the Eel in California and, if I had been alive at the time, I would have thought

Mom crouching at Eel River in California, 1949.

she was hot stuff. While her dad Frank Bell had raised her camping out, riding horses and living in a house heated with wood, she was able to raise us doing many of the same things but with a whole lot less trauma. She grew up hating sleeping on the ground, particularly in the winter, while I grew up to love it. She also engendered a strong sense of compassion and love in us and stood as a shining example of those qualities.

She had that same philosophy and approach to paddling that Ray had instilled in so many: if you ever feel like you are fighting the current, you are probably doing something wrong. You can almost always find a way to get the current to do the work for you. Work with, not against, not only on the river but in life as well. I decided very early that I wanted to work with people and that the golden rule really is the way to live your life.

One of the most important things to learn about and from paddling is when to use speed. As the paddling mentor in residence at Warren Wilson College, I found myself having to explain speed to a bunch of kids who seem to all have attention deficit disorder these days. When I'm teaching I try, whenever possible, to move from the known to the unknown. Analogies are a great way to get across any point. As I thought about speed I tried to come up with something college students would relate to. Knowing when and where to use speed is a lot like...sex! There are definitely times when speed is important, but the rest of the time you just want to chill. Just like sex. A lot of people think that the best way down a rapid is to paddle as fast as you can. That's great if you are racing, but I think there is more to it than that. According to my mother, until Ray came along Chief approached paddling as if he was in a race. Ray introduced a whole other approach to paddling that fused ballet, tai chi and yoga. Slow down, grasshopper. Running a rapid ends all too quickly. You want to savor the experience. Just like sex. Slow down. Catch every eddy, surf every wave. Check out the wildflowers on the bank that only grow in riparian zones. The students have a very mixed reaction to this talk. The girls usually get it and are smiling and the guys are scratching their heads. Speed is essential for certain maneuvers, like getting into and out of eddies. The eddy line typically has currents that flow in opposite directions and it is not a place where you want to hang out. Set your angle, lean and dive across.

When I was a kid growing up at camp, we were using fifteen-foot Grummans that have what is known as a shoe keel on the bottom running the full length of the boat.

We seemed to learn instinctively that the boat would turn better if you leaned dramatically. When we were on the lake working out on the slalom gates, I would always choose a wooden boat. They had no keel and seemed to glide across the water with a lot less effort. We knew the shoe keels were slowing us down in the turns but we did not really appreciate the full extent of what later became known as the "J-lean," where you lean the boat by shifting your weight to a knee and keeping your upper body upright. We just knew that we had to lean those aluminum boats to crank 'em around.

Speed is critical for running drops and punching holes. We knew to line up the drop so we would hit it perpendicularly and hit it fast. We would need a little speed if we were in an eddy and trying to move upstream to get out of the eddy onto a wave to surf it.

As you went around a bend in the current, large or small, if you drift the current is going to push the boat to the outside of the bend. Moving faster than the current and aiming the boat to the high inside of the bend will give control. Pretty much the rest of the time, it was my goal to make it look like I wasn't doing anything. Just like Ray.

Which brings me back to sex. Slow down and savor. I wish somebody had had this talk with me when I was a young man. I just hope that some of these talks I've had with young, impressionable minds has had an impact on some of them.

Teaching paddling has been one of the most rewarding things I have ever done. The more I teach, the more I learn. I am constantly learning from my students and have them to thank for many great learning opportunities. One of the things I struggle with is trying to come up with a different way of explaining something to someone who isn't getting it. This is a lesson that I learned sitting in a wooden canoe on the lake and trying to get some ten-year-olds to understand that when you take a stroke, you are not moving the paddle in the water.

You are simply planting the paddle and using your body to move the boat to the paddle.

My aunt Jane Williams believes that all schools should be built around the barn and there is a lot of truth and wisdom in that belief. My experience has been that a school could actually be built at the canoe docks. I always felt like I learned more in the three months of camp each summer than I learned during the entire nine months of the school year. I was always kind of a dunderhead, but it just seemed like paddling at camp gave me more of the right kind of feedback that I needed to learn about people and the world.

When I was sixteen and starting to go through what my parents envisioned as a "rough" time, my mother's solution was to buy me a used, beat-up old fifteen-foot Grumman from camp and a wetsuit and call David Mason to encourage him to take me paddling. We had some great times and eventually I pulled out of my adolescent funk.

As a teenager, I would always buy a pair of white, canvas deck shoes every year. By the spring, my big toes would be starting to poke through the tops of the shoes, just in time for paddling season at camp. Wearing the shoes in a river environment only hastened the holes' development. Invariably, they would start to fill up with sand in the river environment and become quite uncomfortable. As I would enter a fifteen-foot Grumman, I would lift my feet with the toe angled down to drain the water and sand out. By the end of the summer they would need to be thrown away and the first chore of the new school year was to buy a new pair of deck shoes.

WOODEN CANOES

How I longed for a big Maine birch-bark, such as that which I once went down the Mattawamkeag at high water!
—Teddy Roosevelt, in Candice Millard's The River of Doubt

Wooden canoes. Think about that. Going down a whitewater river in a wooden canoe. Rocks and trees everywhere and you're in a wooden canoe. Scratch a rock and you've got a leak. Trip over. Got to take the boat back to camp and spend most of a day repairing the damage.

Then think about taking a dozen kids down that same river in those wooden canoes. I don't care what anybody today thinks and does, the women and men who were doing this all summer long in the 1920s through the mid-'40s were bold.

Payson Kennedy, former president of the Nantahala Outdoor Center (NOC), wrote a history of paddling section for the book *First Descents*. His research revealed that the Indians of Western North Carolina had dugout canoes, not the remarkable birch bark boats of the Northeast. These dugouts were used predominately to cross the river, not to go down it. The Northeastern birch bark became the forerunner of the more modern wooden and canvas canoes that my family used for camp. The modern wooden and canvas canoes were constructed of ribs and planks, usually cedar wood. They were covered with canvas and weighed around seventy to eighty pounds. I think their wooden construction is beautiful and adds to their spirituality as well as their form. There is nothing that sounds as good as water lapping up against the bottom of a wooden canoe.

Frank Bell—or Chief, his camp name that even I had to use—the director of Camp Mondamin, put in on Mud Creek near Hendersonville, North Carolina, with a small group of campers in 1923 in wooden canoes and they went all the way down the French Broad into the Tennessee River, which flows into the Ohio River before it empties into the Mississippi at Cairo, Illinois. Imagine undertaking a trip of this magnitude during the second year of the camp's existence. This expedition took place before all the dams and lakes were constructed, except the one dam that Chief told Payson Kennedy about in an interview. Today those dams and lakes have come to dominate this river system, stretching all the way to the Mississippi.

As the group descended what is now known as section nine of the French Broad on a day when the river level was up, they encountered what was to be the biggest rapid of the trip. Chief and his camper partner James McClester attempted to run the rapid and ended up in the infamous hole at the bottom. When their boat came out sometime later, all the seats and thwarts had blown out and the boat had completely lost its shape and essentially was destroyed. James was thrown free of the hole, but Chief was re-circulated. He was plunged so deep into the hole that he later developed the belief, based on this experience, that life jackets were a bad idea. He felt that when you get plunged into a hole the way out is to go down as deep as possible to allow the current that exits the hole at the bottom to carry you out, just as he had done

Frank Bell in a Grumman canoe at the lower Keyhole Rapid, in an eddy right above Painted Rock, Chattooga River, 1960s.

that day. Never mind that that is what this hole will do to any boater anyway. I know because I duplicated his swim years later.

I was leading a staff-training trip for Camp Woodson. My partner and I had flipped our canoe above the big hole at the bottom and we struggled to swim the boat to the left shore. As we approached the hole, I realized that we were not going to make it and I used my foot to kick the boat hard to the right, where I knew the ledges broke through in a huge V of current. I did not want to swim the meat of the hole with that big canoe like a tennis shoe in a dryer. I put one hand on top of my head to hold my hat on and the other hand to my glasses, took a deep breath and got plunged deeper than I've ever been plunged. It was dark and surprisingly still. I put my arms out to the side to try to determine what was going on and a flash of a news article headline went through my head: "Frank

41

Bell's Grandson Drowns in Frank Bell's Rapid." Finally I thought I had had enough of this foolishness and started swimming for the surface, which I broke about a hundred feet beyond the hole.

For years, even after Chief's death in 1994, campers were not required to wear life jackets. I grew up at Camp High Rocks not wearing a life jacket on the river, and helmets…well come on, let's get serious. High Rocks didn't get a set of life jackets until the U.S. Forest Service started requiring them on the Chattooga. Once we used them there it became immediately obvious that we would start using them on all rivers. Mondamin, however, continued not to use them for a number of years. The belief was, and it's true, that you learned more about river currents swimming without a life jacket.

We didn't wear life jackets on the lake either; this was something that the insurance companies later would change. When kids first got to camp, they had to go to all the activities and get "qualified." For paddling this meant taking the basic lake test, or BLT. To do this, each camper got in a canoe with a counselor and paddled out onto the lake, where the counselor would turn the boat over, sometimes making a game of "surprising" the scared little kid. After swamping, the camper and the counselor would turn the boat upright and they would hand paddle it back to shore while sitting on the bottom of the boat. The goal was to show campers that the boats float and if they ever turned over on the lake the campers were to stay with the boat. For the counselors this meant a miserable day in the water, and I remember freezing to death, but we were able to feel confident for the rest of the summer that the campers would be all right, even if their boats turned over.

As a camper I can remember holding onto a small loop in a rope and swimming out onto the eddy line at the narrowest point on section three of the Chattooga River in a gorgeous little canyon called the Narrows, and letting the whirlpool on the eddy line suck us down deep into the

Camp High Rocks girls' camp in a Grumman canoe on section three of the Narrows on the Chattooga River, 1964.

river. When we thought we had had enough, we would tug on the rope and about three counselors would pull us to the surface. I don't think we really had a full appreciation, at the time, of just how badly undercut everything is on the Chattooga. Where the rock is undercut beneath the surface, it poses a serious threat as a place to entrap a swimmer.

Chief's reluctance to wear a life jacket eventually gave him a brush with the law. Years later, after the U.S. Forest Service took over the management of boating on the Chattooga, Chief got busted for not wearing a life jacket and he spent years in a protracted legal battle with the Forest Service in Clayton, Georgia.

He owned a little single-engine plane that he used to fly around the country in the winter to promote the camp to parents. He flew kind of recklessly and was known to dive bomb anything he wanted to get a closer look at. Apparently he even crashed his plane in a field once with a camper in it and they walked away from the experience unharmed! He loved a legal battle.

Once he had flown his little plane down to Clayton to fight the U.S. Forest Service and he came to visit us at a little piece of land our family owned that had a ninety-year-old log cabin on it we were restoring. One day we all were walking up a little creek that was on the property. We ascended a small waterfall, and there at the top was an active moonshine still.

Mom had developed a relationship with a wonderful local mountain man and one-time moonshiner named John Henry Nichols, and she called him to tell him to ask those boys to please move their still. On his way back to North Carolina, Chief decided to buzz the area in his plane and Mom became quite concerned that the moonshiners would get nervous and burn our cabin, thinking we may have turned them in to the revenuers. Later that day, we were at the house and I saw two Jeeps with tractor seats bolted to the hoods drive up our little rough, gravel road. Seated on the tractor seats were uniformed men carrying shotguns. Eventually, we heard explosions and the creek started to run a funny color and smelled bad. We had friends who ran a camp nearby and Mom loaded up the whole family to go over to their house until the dust settled. That night we were watching the national news and Dan Rather came on and said that the Bureau of Tobacco, Alcohol and Firearms had rounded up six months of investigations and had destroyed eighty stills in Georgia that day. We went back to the cabin the next day.

During these formative years for Mondamin, a single man contributed more to the camp's paddling program than anybody ever would. John DeLabar ran the canoe docks at camp with a firm but gentle hand. His leadership produced twelve United States and Olympic Team members well after the day that he destroyed two wooden canoes on the Nantahala River on a rapid known since as DeLabar's Rock. As the story goes, he destroyed a wooden canoe on that rock one day. Angrily, he snagged one of the campers' boats and destroyed the second canoe on the same rock. John eventually built a cabin that had no bathroom on Lake Summit. His belief was that if you didn't have a bathroom, visitors wouldn't overstay their welcome. John was a little heavy and one of his favorite things to do was to lash a ladderback chair from the dining hall onto a canoe and paddle with a long, fold boat kayak paddle. Once, John was in charge of a hiking trip that descended a river. His solution to supervision was to float in an inner tube on the river and shout directions to the hiking campers.

My mom, Pat Leverette, said that the flurry of repairs and activity every spring in the boathouse to get the boats ready for the summer was furious. Campers were required to demonstrate superb stokes first on the lake, performing hundreds of dock landings (a maneuver that simulated the combination of strokes required to execute an eddy turn) before they were even allowed to paddle up Lake Summit onto the ripple of the current of the Green River that flowed into the lake, the infamous "Up Green." There they would hone their skills, usually for several years, before they were allowed to make the trip down the mighty lower Green, where famous rapids like Big and Little Corky and Jacobs Ladder waited to test their skills. Campers were even involved in the repair and maintenance of wooden and canvas canoes, an activity that continued to teach the self-reliance and independence skills that were so much a part of everything done at camp.

In Bunny Johns's (former director of the Nantahala Outdoor Center for thirteen years) words,

> When I first went to Camp Merrie Woode, we had a lot of wooden canvases that went on the river and the kids had to, if they put a hole in one, or usually it was just scraping the canvas, they had to repair it. And so they had to sand it down and put the linen sheet there, and then there was the sniffer glue, and then you had to paint it. It was a great experience.

Upper Green River above Lake Summit, Camp Mondamin, 1970s.

Making repairs in the Camp Mondamin boathouse in the 1960s.
Camper Drew Norman is on the left.

On the surface, camp looked like a bunch of fun and games, and it was for the most part. However, everything we did had an educational goal. Personal growth and development, which later became the buzzwords of the adventure education industry, have been practiced at summer camps all over Western North Carolina since the early 1920s, when Frank Bell started his camps.

Mondamin's sessions in those days were eight weeks long, and kids would come back to camp summer after summer. They got really good, and in the years to follow Mondamin turned out a number of United States Paddling Team and Olympic Team members like John Burton, Jamie McEwan and the Haller brothers, Lecki and Fritz. If the campers honed their skills enough, they would qualify for more advanced rivers.

To hone campers' skills on the lake, canoe counselors developed numerous canoe games, like fill-up races, where the object was to use a five-gallon bucket to "fill up" and sink everybody else. Canoe jousting was an activity that Mondamin was famous for, where campers would stand in the bow of a canoe, hold a long padded pole and attempt to "joust" the other camper out of the boat, just like the jousting on horseback of the middle ages.

Camp continued to have a no life jackets policy well into the 1980s. Chief went to his grave in 1994 still convinced that life jackets were a bad idea, and I don't know if he ever resolved his legal battles with the U.S. Forest Service in Clayton, Georgia.

In 1945 Cala Bell (Chief's second wife), who was from Bryson City, North Carolina, returned from a visit home and informed everyone at camp that the government had just built a dam on the Nantahala River near Bryson City that looked like a canoeable stream. Ray went over to the river to have a look-see and he came back very excited. Ray, Pat Bell, Chief, Fritz Orr Sr. (who later founded Camp Merrie Woode), John DeLabar and Billy Pratt from camp went over to Wesser to run the river in wooden canoes. The trip took all day, as they had to

Mom and Ray Eaton in a wooden canoe at Pyramid Rock Rapid on the Nantahala River. This was the first descent of the rapid, in 1945.

scout virtually every rapid to assure safe passage for the wooden canoes.

When they got to the last major rapid, now known as the Nantahala Falls, Ray and Pat Bell, who were in the first boat and were the leaders of the trip, wanted to run the rapid. Chief said, "No, you're not taking my canoes down that." They carried their boats around the rapid, put back on the river and continued the trip. Pat kept encouraging Ray to move faster, as she was concerned that Chief might make them walk another rapid. Ray knew that Big Wesser was down there from having scouted the river fairly extensively from the road and was concerned. That typical dense fog that the Nantahala is famous for had settled on the river and they could hardly see anything. Just as the bow of Ray and Pat's boat almost went over the drop, Pat yelled at Ray that they had to get out of there. Having practiced stern ferries for years, they were able to get to the side and alert the others to pull over before tipping over the edge.

The federal government created Wesser Falls in 1944 when it rerouted the highway that goes by the Nantahala Outdoor Center (NOC) today. Just below NOC, the river used to take a big hairpin turn to river left and the railroad ran over two wooden bridges. When Lake Fontana was built as part of the war effort, workers were faced with building two steel bridges or blasting a channel across the hairpin to straighten the river. Consequently, the rapid is composed of jagged, unnatural rock that makes it a bad decision to run.

In the days when the Nantahala was first run through about the early 1960s, most rapids were negotiated using a series of stern or downstream ferries. This technique is now virtually a forgotten skill, but it was used to move from one side of the river to the other and to negotiate rapids. This was a very elegant way to run rapids, a technique that was largely espoused by Ray. At that time Ray had become the spiritual and emotional leader of Mondamin's paddling program. His talent and wisdom on the river

Ray Eaton crouching with wood and canvas canoe at Eel River in California, 1949.

became the backbone of everything the camp did on the rivers of Western North Carolina. With his long paddle way out to the side, he would vary his stern ferry angle just enough to get the river to do all the work of putting his canoe right where it needed to be. It was inspiring. He used a fairly long paddle because, in those days, he would stand up a lot in order to get a better view of the river downstream. In fact, if you were a real river stud in those days, the hot move was to run Big Corky Rapid on the lower Green River standing on the gunwales of a wooden canoe, a move that Chief was known for. Guys even then were willing to do absurd things to prove their mettle.

Ray was a remarkable man who eventually went on to inspire several camp programs and countless individuals to paddle to greatness. Later, he became the retired senior vice-president of the American Red Cross and the principal negotiator with the North Vietnamese for the release of POWs and MIAs for the United States. He wrote the manual on canoeing for the Red Cross and spent many days at Camps Mondamin, Green Cove, High Rocks, Merrie Woode and the Nantahala Outdoor Center. Ray was a charismatic man with a full shock of flowing white hair. Articulate and soft-spoken, Ray suffered from back problems but continued late in life to paddle with grace, dignity and passion. Many loved and admired him. My mother Pat was one of his favorite paddling partners. Eventually the two of them would go on to pioneer such runs as the Nantahala and take the first guided groups from one of the family camps, High Rocks, down section three of the Chattooga in 1964.

Ray's influence as a diplomat and statesman was made apparent once when he went over to the Nantahala with Merrie Woode and the river had not been turned on by the dam. He jumped on the phone to someone in Washington and before the day was over, the river was turned on and the campers had a great day on the river.

Ray and Chief also had another friend, Ross Allen, who was a remarkable man. Ray had met Ross during his

Ray Eaton and Ross Allen in Florida, 1930s.

times at a camp in Georgia called Camp Athens, where they were campers, along with Fritz Orr Sr. Later Ross ran the Ross Allen Reptile Institute in Silver Springs, Florida. His institute was responsible for providing most of the antivenin to the military during World War II. The springs at Silver Springs were legendary for their clear, gorgeous water and many of the images for the old Red Cross water safety and canoeing texts were shot there. A number of the old Johnny Weissmuller *Tarzan* movies were filmed at Silver Springs, and Ross was a stuntman for Johnny. Silver Springs was home to monkeys that helped the film producers simulate Africa. Sadly, the monkeys have now been eradicated due to health concerns.

Ross collected rattlesnakes and alligators passionately. He and Ray would paddle out into the swamp at night to catch a few gators. Ross stood in the bow of a wooden canoe and Ray paddled. Using headlamps to spot their prey, Ray quietly eased the canoe closer and closer to the

51

American Red Cross lifesaving manual, shot in Silver Springs, Florida, 1950s. Note the fish in the background.

alligator, whose eyes glowed red when spotted by a light. Ross took up a small hank of rope and, from a standing position, dove onto the gator's back out of the canoe. Hopefully the first thing to contact the gator would be Ross's hands around its snout. He would tie the jaws shut and then wrestle the beast into the canoe. They would then paddle their load back to the truck and add it to the institute's growing collection, all in a night's work.

When my sister and I were young, my mom took us down to Florida in the winter to see Ross and paddle some of the amazing springs in the Ocala area near Silver Springs. My introduction to Ross was seeing him walk, with no boots on, into a round concrete pit about three feet deep, full of rattlesnakes. He carried a small snake stick and, after selecting one of the little lovelies, simply turned the snake around, bent over and picked the damned thing up without even pinning the head.

Later we went with him to his alligator farm, which was a row of trailer-like portable cabins out in the swamp. We went on hikes with him and there were numerous areas where he would point out mouse and gopher tortoise dens where rattlesnakes had obviously moved in. Through these areas he instructed us to simply put our feet exactly where he had put his. We were like ducklings right on his tail, very careful to do just as he had instructed. Then we stepped into the water, with alligators and water moccasins everywhere, and it was getting dark. At night when you shined your flashlight into the swamp there were dozens of paired, red eyes. I didn't always sleep restfully when staying on the alligator farm.

Occasionally Ross passed through Camp High Rocks in the summer with a carload of reptiles in special boxes in the back of his station wagon. He would present a reptile show for all the campers who were safely perched on a bank at the top of a little concrete block wall. We would load up to go to the Fletcher Steak House, which was a tradition at camp. As we were driving, we listened to Ross tell stories like the time he was riding down the road and

Fritz Orr Sr. and Ross Allen milking a rattlesnake at Camp Merrie Woode, 1950s.

a giant timber rattler wandered up onto the dash of the car. I'd hear something scratching around behind me in the back and I would sit very still.

As a kid growing up at Camp High Rocks, I would take a wooden canoe down off the racks and paddle out to the slalom gates hanging from a wire strung across a cove. For hours we would practice strokes and maneuvers that we picked up from the U.S. team training and competition films that Ray brought to camp. I remember well when the C-2 team guys started using cross draws in the bow to move to the bow paddler's off side. Until then we had become quite proficient with the pry stoke, an efficient and effective stroke that was gorgeous to watch. Try it on the upstream side on a peel-out or an eddy turn and you'd flip quickly. However, you can ease the paddle into the water, lean hard away from the stroke and you will execute the snappiest turn. This was before the days

Fritz Orr Sr. and Ross Allen with a boa snake at a Camp Merrie Woode reptile show, 1950s.

of thigh straps. I remember nailing effective pries that spun me around in the boat from the forces involved. When the U.S. team started using the cross draw we switched immediately. The cross draw was more stable as you were leaning into the turn, and it's elegant and feels good.

The wooden canoes had no keel and their ability to glide over the water in a turn was much better than the aluminum boats that had a keel. I always felt like the wooden canoes floated on the water like a duck. I never got to paddle a wooden canoe on a river until years later, when Peter White and I decided to enter my mom's old wooden boat, the *Grey Ghost*, in the annual Nantahala downriver race. Of course, we immediately ticked a rock on Patton's Run and cracked the bottom on our practice run. At that point I said, "Race over. We're not going to destroy my mother's prized *Grey Ghost*."

Will Leverette and Peter White in the *Grey Ghost* on the Nantahala River, at the third year of the Outdoorsman Triathlon Race, 1978.

The boat was called the *Grey Ghost* because Mom had the interesting idea of refinishing wooden canoes with silver Grumman aircraft wing dope. She thought that this would be a better finish; that eventually turned out not to be true, but it made for a beautiful canoe. Pete and I did compete in the Nantahala race that year, and my former wife Lee got a pretty good picture of us coming down through Patton's Run before we damaged the canoe. Patton's Run is the first rapid on the standard Nantahala run. Bob Benner, who later wrote the guidebook to the rivers of North Carolina, named it for Charlie Patton because of Charlie's tireless and excellent devotion to teaching paddling.

Typically a rapid is named for someone who had an epic screw-up on the drop years ago. Patton's Run was previously known as the First Rapid on the Nantahala, but sometime in the early 1970s Bob began to call it Patton's Run as a tribute to Charlie. Charlie was a World War II veteran with a badly damaged arm who was also a postman from Brevard, North Carolina. Several of his C-1s (one-person decked boats) were at camp.

That experience that Pete and I had cracking the *Grey Ghost* on Patton's Run left me with respect for what running a camping whitewater program must have been like many years ago. The kids had to be so well prepared and the rivers that were run had to be well within their skill level. Things have changed today with plastic boats, rock splats and boofing maneuvers, where hitting rocks is the goal.

The age of the wooden canoe on Southern whitewater rivers may be over, but there are a few of us still around who remember well the sight of a wooden canoe expertly steered by a well-trained tandem team of kids who grew up at camp. Learning how to paddle in wood prepared a lot of people to later take aluminum and then plastic to new heights.

I always felt like having learned how to paddle in wood gave me an edge over other paddlers who never

High/brace draw, wood and canvas canoe at Camp Green Cove,
Lake Summit, 1940s.

paddled in wooden boats. In retrospect, I was probably
deceiving myself, but I do believe that the experience was
a valuable component of my paddling education. Ray
always chose a wooden boat for his daily evening paddle
around the perimeter of the lake at camp, something I
will never forget.

ALUMINUM CANOES AND
FIBERGLASS BOATS

*Only those who have the patience to do simple things perfectly ever
acquire the skills to do difficult things easily.*
−*John C. Shilling*

The wooden era of whitewater canoeing came to
a grateful end after the Second World War, when
Grumman Aircraft began to make aluminum canoes.
A Grumman executive, William Hoffman, had been
portaging a heavy wooden boat in the Adirondacks
when he had the idea that it was time for Grumman to
make the transition from wartime production to more
peaceful pursuits. Eventually, Grumman hired a young
man named John Achilich, who designed the fifteen-
and seventeen-foot models we have come to know and
love. Eventually Grumman sold 300,000 boats, peaking
in 1974 with sales of 33,000 as a result of the popularity
of the movie *Deliverance*.

Gone were the days of furious wooden canoe repair
in the spring in preparation for the arrival of campers
in June. Gone were the days of preparation of campers
who could keep the boats off the rocks, although the
better camps like Mondamin, Green Cove, High Rocks

and Merrie Woode continued to demand excellent boat control from their little darlings.

Aluminum was very durable and could be left out in the weather all winter long. Sure, when someone wrapped a canoe around a rock, it was really stuck. You haven't lived until you've tried to unpin an aluminum canoe. They can wrap themselves around a rock like a piece of tinfoil, and let's not even talk about the noise. When you hit a rock in an aluminum canoe, what you just did is loudly announced to the world. We used to laugh and joke and call it thunder.

Aluminum also has a nasty habit of sticking to rocks and so, by the middle of summer, as the river water levels started to drop, we would actually smear car wax on the bottom of the boats in preparation for a trip. This seemed to help the boats slide off the rocks a little better. Or at least that's what we thought.

The hull designs of the Grummans were actually not that great, but they represented a huge advancement over wooden canoes. Over time—more than ten years—the hull of a Grumman can actually take more abuse than a plastic canoe; just don't wrap the thing around a rock.

Sometime in the 1970s we started carrying throw ropes. In the early days, when someone stuck an aluminum canoe on a rock, my other paddling counselor and I would first collect the paddlers and their paddles. Then one of us would wade or swim out to the pinned boat to free it. This often would involve a combination of pulling and pushing, prying with small logs found in the woods and figuring out which end had more current to help you move the boat. Campers were never allowed to assist in this effort due to the hazards involved. Sometimes the other counselor could work his or her way out to assist, but typically I did it by myself. Once the boat was freed, I would grab a painter (the ropes tied to both ends of a canoe) and swim the boat to the end of the rapid, where I could then swim it to shore.

John DeLabar standing on the rocks at the second drop of the Toxaway Narrows, 1950s.

After we started carrying ropes, the whole process became immeasurably easier. I would go out to the pinned boat with the rope, secure the line to the boat and throw the end to shore. Then, after the boat was freed, it could be swung to shore easily by the group. We thought we were hot stuff.

The first time I paddled the Nantahala in 1968, the camp leaders took us up to the bridge that goes over the river right below the power plant that is just upstream of the point where the natural side of the Nantahala and the water from the power plant join. First-time initiation was a very daunting task for a scared little twelve-year-old boy. We had to jump into the water off the bridge and swim about a hundred yards downstream to the confluence of the natural side. The Nantahala's water is drawn from the bottom of the deepest lake in North Carolina and the temperature of the water starts in the low fifties and, in the course of the eight-

and-a-half-mile run, warms up to a balmy sixty-three degrees. When I hit the drink off the bridge, my first impression was that it really hurt my Adam's apple. I swam as fast as I could down to the confluence with the natural side and jumped in the warmer waters. It felt balmy, which is remarkable given the typically cool nature of most mountain streams. Today, the U.S. Forest Service has established a parking area and a put-in just downstream for private boaters, and nobody in their right mind jumps off that bridge.

The skill and responsibility of a camp paddling counselor were enormous in years gone by. During girls' camp I might have a group of little girls and one assistant adolescent female counselor. Not much muscle power, in other words.

One time I was driving the camp truck towing a trailer loaded with seven canoes, twelve paddlers and about twelve tubers up the old, dirt road coming out of the Green River when I took one of the seventeen hairpin turns too tight. The rear wheels immediately sank in the loose, dusty dirt. I tried to back up to get out of my predicament, and immediately jackknifed the trailer. I unloaded all the starving little girls and enlisted the help of my assistant to unhook the trailer and back it down the road. I then backed the truck down to the trailer, hooked it up and loaded the girls back up and drove them back to camp just in time for dinner. Just another day on the job, and we got to do it all over again the next day and for the rest of the summer. I loved it.

Early paddling pioneers logged many first descents and some epics were experienced. Pat Leverette, my mom, working as the head of paddling for High Rocks girls' camp, led one of the most interesting early trips. A popular run for many years—until Lake Jocassee put it under water in 1973—was known as the Keowee River. The actual river that everyone was thinking about, however, was the Toxaway and it flowed into the Keowee, a more tranquil run that camp used for beginners. The

The Camp Green Cove truck and trailer were built by camp maintenance man H. Allen on a 1953 Willy's Jeep axle loaded with wood and canvas canoes, post 1945.

Chief in an aluminum canoe at Toxaway Narrows, 1960s.

run had a beautiful section called the Narrows that was characterized by giant slabs and wonderful rapids.

Once, in the early sixties, my mom had taken a group of girls over there from Camp High Rocks. The drive to this area of the mountains (now known as the Gorges) in those days was quite long from Cedar Mountain and ended on logging roads. The group made camp on the banks of the river at the put-in and settled in for a night of continuous rain. It rained so hard that the river began to rise.

In the middle of the night, Terrell Garrard, a camper, heard the bundle of wooden paddles that she had made and stacked against a tree tumble over. She got up and saw that the river was in their campsite! They moved their shelters back and settled into their sleeping bags for what remained of the night, only to be woken up again by the rising river. They moved camp again and woke up in the morning to a flooded river.

Mom said, "Too bad. We'll have to drive back to camp. We're not paddling today."

The girls mutinied. "We came all this way and we've got to paddle. Please, please, please," they begged. Mom groaned.

She didn't really want to make the drive, and part of her reluctance was due to two of the many challenges that faced a camp counselor in those days: long drives and carsick kids. We used a big flatbed pickup truck with a canvas cover over the back and benches for the campers to sit on (not exactly legal later on, and for a good reason). Fortunately, we never had any serious problems. Invariably one or more of the kids would become carsick and start spewing the contents of their breakfast of sausage patties and stewed apples all over everybody, and once that smell got started others were soon to follow. The group had driven all that way and really didn't want to drive the long haul back. Mom tried to hold her ground but eventually she acquiesced and they put on the river. That was the first mistake.

Camp Green Cove campers in a Grumman canoe at Toxaway Narrows, 1960s.

In no time at all, they entered the Narrows and the shitake hit the fan. Boats were all over the place and a number of the group got separated onto an island. Mom had turned over as well and her partner experienced a head-up foot entrapment. Any kind of an entrapment is serious, but at least this girl was breathing. Concerned about the part of the group that had washed up on the island and was separated, Mom made sure the entrapped girl was fundamentally okay, left her there and hit the bank to count heads. When she knew that everyone was all right, she returned to the girl who was stuck in the river. With some finagling and one lost tennis shoe, the camper was freed. They then rejoined the group. The only problem was that someone had lost a boat.

Rufus Bethea was the shuttle driver of the trip and he had been pacing the shore wondering where the group was. He narrowly avoided stepping on a rattlesnake and looked up to see an empty, swamped boat floating down the river. Rufus dove in the river without hesitation to retrieve the boat and wondered what had happened.

Meanwhile, the group had "doubled up" and put three campers in several of the boats. They arrived at the take-out on the Keowee and were very happy to see Rufus. Mom was greatly relieved and would go to her grave with the sense that she had exercised the poorest judgment of her paddling career that day. In fact, from that day on she never led a canoeing trip again and became a silversmith and pottery counselor in the craft shop instead.

About the same time, Mom and Ray took a group of girls from High Rocks down section three of the Chattooga. Hugh Caldwell, a Sewanee professor and amazing early, difficult river pioneer from Camp Merrie Woode, had already run the river sometime in the early 1950s, alone in an eighteen-foot aluminum canoe. He had run sections two and three in one day and he had no real idea what was down there; he used a Gulf Oil road map as his only guide. Lots of people have done amazing things for many years, but I consider this feat to be one of the most spectacular.

Randy Carter in an aluminum canoe at Slide Rapid on the Toxaway River, 1950s.

Bunny Johns remembers Hugh and his contribution to Camp Merrie Woode well:

> *I can still see Hugh, he's got on a felt hat, got his pipe in his mouth; he was a philosophy professor at Sewanee, University of the South. He was the caricature of a philosophy professor. He was out there* [laugh], *but he spent every summer, long before I went there and long after I left, he did his summers at Merrie Woode teaching kids how to canoe, and because of who he was, he was a philosopher and he also had a mathematical background, he made the kids understand why the strokes worked—equal and opposite reaction forces and all that kind of stuff—and so if you were going to be a captain, which was a big deal, you had to learn some theory along with the actual strokes.*

I'm sure Hugh and Ray communicated and I'll bet that's how Ray found out about section three. Pat and Ray had a fairly uneventful day on the river with the

Camp High Rocks campers in a Grumman canoe on section three of the Chattooga River, Warwoman Rapid, 1964.

group, partly because they were so well trained. At the bottom of Dick's Creek, below what is now known as the First Ledge, the group spied a big buck deer wading.

At the end of the river there is a notorious rapid called Bull Sluice, which apparently is not the original Bull Sluice. The real Bull Sluice is under the waters of Lake Tugaloo, below section four. Today's Bull Sluice is a big, long, class-four drop that has a nasty ledge and a wide hole near the bottom.

Ray knew that the rapid existed but didn't know exactly where it was. Sumner Williams, the director of Camp High Rocks, was the shuttle driver that day. A fairly accomplished paddler himself, Sumner had not been able to join the trip, as he had just dropped a log on his knee with a chain saw and was rehabilitating. He knew that the Bull was there and he had hobbled on crutches up the river to the rapid to warn the group. It was getting dark and the group came around the bend in the river to see Sumner standing on the shore waving one of his crutches to warn them. The sand where Sumner had been was riddled with pockmarks from his crutches. The campers carried their boats around the drop, just as we did for many years.

To this day, section three remains the highlight of a camper's summer. To make the section three trip is quite a badge of honor and descending it is a very big event for a camper. Mike Stevenson, who later ran the paddling program at camp and was on that early descent of section three, used to take us down the river. We would spend so much time swimming and playing on the river that we would invariably run out of time. All those undercut rocks made for some interesting swimming opportunities. There's a ledge right at the bottom of the First Ledge, or Dick's Creek Ledge, that is, like most of the drops on the Chattooga, very undercut. It's a big, spectacular clamshell that we used to take great pleasure in swimming up under, where we could actually breathe and stick our arms out as other paddlers passed by and

Will Leverette and Susan Sherrill (later Grant) at Bull Sluice on the
Chattooga River, 1980.

wave madly as if we were trapped. We always finished
in near darkness and went to the Walhalla Steak House
for a dinner of fried chicken. Then we would go back
to camp in the darkness with the lights turned off as we
crested the last hill, so as to not wake up the campers.
We did that every summer.

In a parallel development, several staff from the
Nantahala Outdoor Center—including Bunny Johns,
who was a former Merrie Woode camper and later
counselor (Bunny went on to become the president of
NOC and a World Cup gold medallist)—teamed up with
Hugh Caldwell and Fritz Orr Jr. to go down to Clayton,
Georgia, to paddle section four of the Chattooga in 1964
for the first time. Everyone on the trip was highly skilled,
which made the trip go very smoothly. Until they got to
the Five Falls, that is. This spectacular area of rapids
is characterized by a series of five cascades that, when

Fritz Orr Jr. and Fritz Orr Sr. paddling in an aluminum canoe on the Nantahala Falls of the Nantahala River, 1950s.

viewed from the bottom, constitutes the single most impressive series of drops in the Southeast, or possibly the country. They scare me silly.

The first rapid, called Entrance, is a mellower class-four introduction to what is to come in the next several hundred yards. The second rapid is called Corkscrew, which fairly accurately describes what happens to my stomach about this time in the descent. One of the hard truths of paddling is that you must be able to visualize yourself performing the moves to successfully negotiate passage. If you can't see yourself paddling the rapid, trust me, you can't do it. Corkscrew is such a convoluted, violent mess that I simply can't see myself getting down it without having serious problems. Therefore, I usually walk this one. Because of my MS, I can't even struggle my way down Sneakscrew, which is the sneak route (a move that I am typically proud to make on most rapids).

The next big falls is Crack in the Rock, a six-foot vertical drop that has three breaks where the river pours through. Left Crack is a killer and has claimed the lives of several people since that epic descent of 1964. Middle Crack had a giant log pointing up at the sky for years and was consequently not runnable. Right Crack presents the fewest problems, but is unpleasant enough that the three raft companies that run the river today still do not take customers down it or any other crack. Between Corkscrew and Crack, by this time, most paddlers' butts are bound up like they have been taking pain meds for a month.

Jawbone is next and I see the line on this one, although it's very intimidating due to the gigantic rock three-quarters of the way down that is so badly undercut that it has claimed the lives of several people who have had the bad luck of getting tangled up in the debris of logs that get lodged under it. It is called Hydroelectric Rock, and if you aren't wound up tighter than a manifold spring on a '56 Chevy by now then you are either dead or a bigger whitewater stud than me.

Bunny and Hugh's group had either portaged or successfully run its way down section four to this point when Fritz Orr Jr. attempted to load up his canoe and pulled one of those unexplained mistakes and turned his boat over. He lost control of the swamped boat and could not recover to shore before it washed over the next rapid, a huge ten-foot drop called Sock 'Em Dog. Fritz was able to get to shore but his boat took the plunge. Despite exhaustive efforts to recover the sunken craft, the group was unable to find it. It was gone, and even when they returned the next day with grappling hooks, they were still unable to get a sounding of hook to aluminum. To this day, no one knows what happened to that boat. It may still be pinned under an undercut for all we know. Fortunately, several of the party were paddling solo and Fritz had a boat to crawl into to get out of there.

The river goes through one more semi-serious rapid, called Shoulder Bone, before it hits the tranquil waters of Lake Tugaloo, where Fritz Orr Sr. had motorboated

Bunny Johns and Dawn Benner in a C-2 at Second Ledge on the Chattooga River, 1980.

up the two-mile lake section to pick up the group. From a distance he could count boats and knew that something had happened. According to the United States Forest Service records, from 1970 to 1980 twenty-three people have drowned on the Chattooga River, a grisly legacy. Fortunately, no one made the record books that day.

In 1971 we began to explore a relatively untested river, the Nolichucky, near Erwin, Tennessee. Several counselors from camp had run it and came back with stories of big rapids and a beautiful gorge. Six of us campers had been coming back to camp summer after summer and we had gotten pretty good. Bill Doswell, the designated "old fart" of the day, decided that we should run it.

Jack McCallie of Chattanooga, Tennessee, and I had been on a hiking trip at camp and had become instant buddies. I talked him into becoming a boater and for the next ten years we were inseparable. If we spotted someone on the shore who was pointing a camera at us, we would instantly become the biggest hams in the world, singing camp songs like "Jump Down, Turn Around" and "Mountain Dew." Something happens to kids at camp when these bonds get formed. An attachment begins that can become a lifelong friendship. Jack and I are still very close, even though we don't see each other very often.

When we arrived at the put-in for the Nolichucky, the river was flooded and was running 3.2 feet, the biggest I've ever seen it (median flow is 1.4 feet). The color told us it was big and swollen, but we had no idea just how pumped up it was. Bill had, fortuitously, already decided that we needed to be loaded for bear and we took 17-foot Grummans with giant truck tubes jammed and tied in the center for additional flotation.

The shuttle ran up a fairly steep dirt road that had the worst washboards I have ever seen. The drive took one and a half hours to make one way and contributed to the buildup of what running the Nolichucky was all about. By the time we actually put in the river, our adolescent minds were chomping at the bit. However, in no time at all we were quickly humbled by the power of a flooded river. We had a real eye-opener of a day, but did just fine on the rapids we didn't carry around, which were quite a few.

The first rapid starts below a railroad bridge that you encounter within a couple hundred yards of the put-in. In typical Bill Doswell fashion, our three camper and three counselor boats eddy-hopped down the far right side of the run, which kept us out of the big water in the middle. The second rapid comes up right away and we chose to scout it on the left bank. One look at the monster that is called On the Rocks convinced us that we would be walking around this one on the left. This was probably the first time that I got my taste of scouting a rapid simply to decide where I was going to carry the boat.

We put back on and proceeded through a wonderful rock garden until the top of a long rapid not too much farther downstream called Quarter Mile. We were able to pick our way down this tumultuous section with no mishaps, one at a time. It's probably a good thing that we were not more seasoned and didn't have better judgment, although, looking back, I have to question the judgment of our leaders (I don't want to mention any names for fear of embarrassing their parents, Mr. and Mrs. Doswell and Mrs. Mason). On numerous drops we filled up with water and had to bail out, laughing hysterically, but no one actually turned over.

As we eddy-hopped our way downstream, we exercised tremendous caution and proceeded carefully. At one point it had started to rain again and Bill stopped us on one of those classic, big sandy Nolichucky beaches as we were starting to get cold. In those days we didn't even know what a paddling jacket was, much less carry them, so we spent a few minutes running up and down the beach to build some warmth. The Nolichucky is a long eleven miles. We finished and pulled out at a railroad bridge that is about a mile downstream of the current take-out. We were getting pretty good at this river running stuff and later, in the next few years, did some pretty spectacular runs like Wilson Creek and Big Laurel Creek, which were way ahead of our time but within our skill level.

Also in the early 1970s, a number of us happened to show up at the same time at camp with fiberglass kayaks, European racing boats like Prions and Lettmans that we bought on the used boat market. In those days you could buy a used, leaky fiberglass boat for a hundred dollars.

I remember learning how to execute an Eskimo roll by having my cousin David Williams show me the stroke over and over without turning over until I about got it right. He then told me to flip and "just do that stroke," which is what I did and I rolled right back up on my first attempt!

After a kid learns how to paddle a canoe, paddling a kayak is pretty easy and I had been paddling canoes since I was seven. To this day, campers are required to learn canoeing first before they even get into a kayak. Teaching rolling to these kids is a real ego boost, as it's pretty easy to do.

Aluminum Canoes and Fiberglass Boats

The night before a big river trip was usually spent repairing fiberglass, a throwback to the old days of wooden canoe repairs before a trip. Those fiberglass racing boats really opened up a whole new world to us. Rivers like section four of the Chattooga, the Ocoee and the Nolichucky became our playgrounds. We were learning, running new rivers and loving it.

Eddy Weatherby, Martin Begun and Hugh Caldwell of Camp Merrie Woode got bitten hard by the paddling bug and began to make many first descents doing what was later to be known as "creekin'." One day, in 1973, they ran the Green River Narrows. It was a beautiful day and both units (or "flumes," as we called them in those days) were running. They put in at the power plant and were paddling fiberglass boats; Eddy in a fiberglass Pavelbone kayak and Martin in a Hahn C-1. At some point, Eddy cracked the end of his boat off in a vertical pin situation. He went into the woods and found a log about the size

Martin Begun, a Merrie Woode paddling counselor, in an old Hahn design C-1, at the first descent of Potter Falls on the Tellico River in Tennessee.

of the broken end, stuffed it into the boat and duct taped it in place. They finished the trip convinced that this run would never become a popular one, so they loaded their boats, went over to the Chattooga and ran sections zero and one.

In the early 1970s, Jamie McEwan, former Mondamin boy and later 1972 Olympic C-1 bronze medallist, ran the Linville Gorge with his brother Tommy for what was probably the first descent of that river.

Jimmy Holcombe and David Benner were working at NOC in the 1970s and were beginning to run steep creeks all over Western North Carolina in fiberglass boats. Running little, steep, gradient creeks became the thing to do and is, to this day, what North Carolina whitewater boating is famous for.

In the early seventies five things happened to change the sport forever. The movie *Deliverance* was released and all of a sudden every Tom, Dick and Harry in Atlanta wanted to be Burt Reynolds. If you bought a case of Coke in Atlanta, you got a free cheapy raft. In the first three years after the movie came out, nineteen people drowned on the Chattooga. Later we learned that Payson Kennedy of the Nantahala Outdoor Center, Claude Terry and Doug Woodward (who later founded a raft company called Southeastern Expeditions) had been used as stuntmen for the film. Little did we appreciate the significance and impact that this film would have on "our rivers." To this day the local people in Clayton hate *Deliverance* for how they were portrayed, which was not always in a complimentary light. According to Doug Woodward in his wonderful book, *Wherever Water Flows*, Jon Voight and Ned Beatty were very approachable and Burt Reynolds was not. The locals of Rabun County do not hold Reynolds, even now, in very high esteem.

Secondarily, whitewater premiered in the Olympics in 1972 in Augsburg, Germany, and all of a sudden, between *Deliverance* and the Olympics, whitewater was in the public's consciousness and things would never be the same again. Several Mondamin boys, like John Burton, Tom Southworth and Jamie McEwan, were on the Olympic team because they were national champions and members of the United States Team. Jamie got a bronze medal in C-1 (a one-person decked canoe that is paddled with a single bladed paddle), the United States' only Olympic medal in whitewater events until the 1992 Olympics in Barcelona, Spain, where Tennessee's Joe Jacobi and Scott Strausbaugh won gold medals in C-2 (a two-person decked boat where both paddlers use single blades), along with Dana Chladek's bronze in women's slalom.

Third on my list of significant developments was that the Nantahala Outdoor Center (NOC) was founded on the Nantahala River in 1972. NOC became the preeminent school for thousands of people to get instruction for developing whitewater skills and to run the world-famous Western North Carolina rivers. About 300,000 people a year go down the Nantahala now, making the river the most popular whitewater in the country.

The fourth thing that happened was that Bill Masters and Perception Kayaks started making plastic canoes and kayaks in Easley, South Carolina, in 1976, although he had begun to make boats for his friends around 1972 in his garage. Before 1972, if we saw someone on the river, we either knew them or someone they knew who was affiliated with one of the four camps. I was running the Nantahala with High Rocks one time as a camper in the early seventies when the counselors decided to get their chilled fannies off the river, as it had been raining hard all day. We pulled out at what was then the Gorgerama Rock Swap Shop a short ways above the Nantahala Falls and NOC. A man wielding a pistol came out of a trailer and ordered us to get back on the river, which we did. Now there are signs on the river right above there that invite boaters to stop for hot coffee, pizza and hot dogs. When Perception, Blue Hole and Mad River began to produce plastic canoes

Camp Merrie Woode at section two of the Chattooga River. Notice the Jimmy and Rosalyn Carter inscription.

in the early seventies that anybody thought they could paddle, things really took off. All of a sudden there were lots of people on the river who we didn't know.

Finally, the Wild and Scenic Rivers Act got its start in 1968 and the Chattooga got its first taste of federal protection in 1974 by being officially included in the act. The Chattooga was the first river east of the Mississippi designated "wild and scenic," with forty of the river's fifty-seven miles designated as wild, two as scenic and fifteen as recreational. That protection has endured a checkered history. The local people on the South Carolina side have mostly adhered to the regulations and safeguards that the government put into place, but many fishermen have not been happy.

The U.S. Forest Service does not allow vehicles any closer than half a mile from the river, except for the paved road accesses at the start of section two (Long Bottom Ford) and the take-out for section three (Highway 76) right below Bull Sluice, which are old access points that have been there for a long time. Local river users have had free reign on the river for many years and they didn't like the new restrictions. In fact, they threatened to burn down the forest in the seventies if the Forest Service chose to enforce the new rules. The Forest Service has capitulated and to this day does not enforce its access policies on the Georgia side, a fact that I find amazing. I've seen people driving their pickup trucks into the river at Sandy Ford on section three and washing them with soapy water next to the broken beer bottles that litter the shore, all in a federally protected river basin.

At first, I felt I had to assist in the rescue of the masses of inexperienced people who obviously had no clue about safety and especially self-rescue. After about a season of this foolishness I decided that unless the rescue involved a head-under situation, I was not going to be responsible for knuckleheads who got into a little trouble. I suppose this can cut both ways, as I am often hitchhiking my shuttle, especially on a popular river like the Nantahala, and sometimes I'll be standing there with a life jacket on and boaters will actually pass me by! Fortunately, this doesn't happen very often and people are usually willing to pick up an obvious boater.

We have come to learn to live with the increased traffic on "our rivers" and can only hope that these people are voters who may remember their beautiful day on the river when it comes time to cast their voice with regard to water quality and access issues. I hope that raft guides are taking the opportunity with their customers to stump water quality and other important river issues with the public. The river experience is so much more than a thrill ride at a water park and until the public joins us in the political process, we may continue to lose access and water quality will continue to deteriorate. American Whitewater really is the best organization to join in this regard, and every boater in the country should be a member. It's cheap and they do the best job of promoting issues that are the most important to boaters. I'll get off my soapbox. Join.

Plastic boats quickly became popular because of their user-friendly hulls. Bob Benner, the first author of a guidebook for Western North Carolina rivers, called them grease boats because of their increased ability to slide off obstructions. Rocks in the rivers we frequented usually had some silver color, rubbed off from the aluminum era. Increasingly, a rainbow of colors has replaced this silver. One of the more popular rapids on section three of the Chattooga is called Painted Rock (aka Key Hole) because of the coloration that has rubbed off from decades of unskilled boaters' crafts.

Flotation devices for canoes also underwent a big transformation. For a number of years the Nantahala Outdoor Center used big blocks of Styrofoam in its canoes. You would actually see little piles of chipped Styrofoam floating in the eddies of popular rivers like the Nantahala. Inflatable float bags have largely replaced the Styrofoam. You don't see Styrofoam floating on the river anymore.

At Camp Mondamin my cousin, David Williams, learned paddling as an artistic expression as well as being serious about having good clean fun on the river. He combined an interesting mix of hard skills and philosophy. David used to take his classes from Camp High Rocks down the lower Green River. As in most of the lower Green beginner classes, the trip would start with everyone getting into the put-in pool without life jackets and swimming in the current to develop a feel for moving water. To know that swimming in current is not necessarily a dangerous thing is an essential skill for budding whitewater enthusiasts. David always said, "Establishing a relationship with the river is born first out of swimming without a life jacket."

As the trip progressed down the river, campers were asked to stop and learn a few skills before they could move on. On selected, usually class-two rapids, campers had to first demonstrate that they could run the rapid

Camp Green Cove/Camp Mondamin counselor Bill Adams deflecting potential rock impact in a Grumman canoe at Toxaway Narrows, 1960s.

paddling on either side and then in either position—bow or stern. Then, if it were appropriate, everyone would swim the rapid.

David's clearest memories of the Toxaway Narrows were that it wasn't terribly difficult, just swift. One of the most fun things to do was to swim the whole Narrows, shelves, ledges, shoals and big potholes that characterize this stream. This river, as any river, had a very distinct personality and characteristics that set it apart from any other. The Toxaway Narrows had its own feel and look that separated it from the typical mountain stream that was filled with boulders and rocks, like the Nantahala. The potholes on the Narrows were big and well developed enough that there were several where a camper could swim a tunnel inside the rocks all the way through from the top to the bottom.

81

The classic South Carolina streams—the Chattooga, Toxaway and the Chauga—are very similar even though each, like most rivers, has its own identity. The Chauga had a lot of big slides that were shallow and reminiscent of Sliding Rock on the Davidson River headwaters in Pisgah National Forest near Brevard, North Carolina.

One time I was running the Chauga as a camper when we pulled over at the bottom of one of those big slides. Oftentimes we could line up the initiation of the drop, but once we tipped over the edge and began the slide, it was all you could do to hope that you landed in the pool at the bottom upright, as there wasn't enough water to take a stroke.

Once Bob Benner was running the lower Green River and he encountered some campers from Camp Green Cove at the bottom of Little Corky Rapid. The girls were skinny-dipping in the river and one of the girls cussed Bob out for having surprised them. Bob did not dawdle and his little group continued downstream.

In the mid-1960s David and another camp counselor, Pat Stone, heard about a new river, the Nolichucky, from the Merrie Woode great, Hugh Caldwell. Hugh had scouted the river from the railroad that runs the length of the river canyon. David and Pat paddled seventeen-foot Grummans solo, as they had done on many trips, including section four of the Chattooga. David and Pat were doing what is now known as leapfrogging. This is a technique where one boat goes ahead to scout the drop and then waves the second boat through the best route. The second boater runs the drop to where he can stop, scout the next drop and wave or yell to the first boater where to go.

This descent in 1968 was the first time anyone from our family's camps had run this river and may have been the first time anyone had run the Nolichucky. This was true of many of the early descents. Who knows? Looking back, the river could well have been paddled before, but as far as we knew, this was the first. It doesn't matter and Dave and Pat were heroes in our minds.

Aluminum Canoes and Fiberglass Boats

Bob Benner was one of the earliest, if not the first, pioneer of the Nolichucky and he named several of the prominent rapids on the run, such as On the Rocks and Quarter Mile. He probably was among the first paddlers of some of the classics like Wilson Creek and Big Laurel Creek. Benner also named Stairstep on the Big Laurel. He took a Sierra Club group down section nine of the French Broad, where he gave Big Pillow its name sometime in the early 1970s. Years later I tried to find out who had named the now-famous rapids of the Chattooga. The best story I've been able to get is that the names were Indian in origin and the Five Falls on the Chattooga were already named by the time people began to paddle them. A number of names get used over and over on rivers, like the Narrows. There is a Narrows on the Toxaway, the Green and the Chattooga, and there is an Accelerator on the Pigeon as well as the Ocoee.

Randy Carter, author of *Canoeing Whitewater River Guide*, was probably the first person to paint gauges on bridge pilings, and Bob Benner soon followed his lead to give boaters some kind of a reference to the water levels. Once Bob established zero on the gauge, usually low water, he would talk to local boaters to get further information. Levels above and below zero and their significance would then be recorded in the book. Truthfully, Bob and his son David incorporated some guesswork and some checking of levels relative to the base level. Bob published the second guide to Western North Carolina whitewater rivers, *Carolina White Water: A Paddlers Guide to the Western Carolinas*, to give paddlers a reference to runnable rivers and their appropriate water levels.

There was a lot of resentment amongst most of the people I boated with from camp when NOC first came into being. We considered the Nantahala to be our river and NOC brought the crowds. Looking back, it wasn't just NOC that meant changes for "our river." The introduction of whitewater into mainstream America was as much about the interesting combination of factors that came together in 1972 as it was about NOC's appearance. The movie *Deliverance* and whitewater's debut in the Olympics had much to do with the explosion of interest in boating, as did the building of NOC. Had we been more aware of everything that was happening, we would have been grateful that it was NOC and not some bunch of money-hungry, raft company yahoos that ended up on "our river." At least Payson Kennedy and the people who created NOC shared our love and respect for the river. We would have to learn to live with the public and respect their right to be there as much as our rights and history.

Plastic Canoes
and Kayaks

Soon our boats reach the swift current; a stroke or two, now on this side, now on that and we thread the narrow passage with exhilarating velocity, mounting the high waves, whose foaming crests dash over us, and plunging into the troughs, until we reach the quiet water below; and then comes a feeling of great relief.
—John Wesley Powell,
The Exploration of the Colorado River, *1869*

In 1971 there was a little fishing supply store and Esso gas station in Wesser, North Carolina, on the Nantahala River called the Tote-N-Tarry Hotel Restaurant and Gas Station. The Nantahala had built a limited reputation for itself as an excellent trout fishing stream, partly due to its isolation and partly due to the cold, clear water that flowed down it from high in the mountains out of the Nantahala Lake that promoted the well-being of fish.

Several of Western North Carolina's summer camps for children had discovered the river as an excellent, quiet playground for whitewater canoeing as far back as 1945. Hundreds of campers from camps like Merrie Woode, High Rocks, Mondamin and Green Cove had been led to discover the river's beauty and frighteningly cold water, sometimes the hard way. Still, the traffic on the river consisted mostly of fishermen and the occasional summer camp paddling program.

Once camp had closed for the season at the end of the summer, all the campers went back to their homes and the next winter's school year. Traffic on the river dwindled to a trickle and almost no boaters were seen until the next summer. How the Tote-N-Tarry stayed in business is amazing.

In 1972 a man from Atlanta named Horace Holden, who owned a summer camp in northern Georgia, bought the Tote-N-Tarry for a place he could bring his campers to. He convinced a friend of his, Payson Kennedy, a librarian at Georgia Tech, and his wife Aurelia to manage the fledgling business. They quickly came up with the name—the Nantahala Outdoor Center—and began the task of building a business. Who would have guessed that that business would become the largest employer in the county in twenty years and set the standards by which all outdoor guide services would be measured?

At first, NOC used aluminum Grumman canoes. In 1974 Bob Lance, Don Dial and Roy Guinn founded the Blue Hole Canoe Company in Sunbright, Tennessee, named for the Blue Hole on Mill Creek behind the shop where the first boats were produced. Blue Holes were generic pools on rivers where boaters could rest and enjoy the riparian environment. The superiority of the Blue Hole Canoe was immediately apparent and in no time that boat became the dominant design on the river. NOC became the biggest dealer and began to put large Styrofoam blocks in the center of the boat for flotation, and suddenly everybody in the country had a boat they could get down the river in without wrapping it around a rock. In 1974 the Open Canoe Nationals Race was held on the Nantahala River and Blue Hole loaned boats to whomever wanted to use them in the race. Ultimately, over 50 percent of the races' winners paddled the new boat, including Bob Lantz and his son Bobby, who took second in the Jr./Sr. slalom event. The impact that the Blue Hole Canoe had on the industry cannot be overestimated. I even had one, although I refused to use those heavy Styrofoam blocks for flotation. I used two smaller chunks of Styrofoam in the ends and a big truck inner tube stuffed into the middle and blown up until it almost popped; I was old school and proud of it. I even recently found out from Bob that that was the same thing that he used in his boat.

Horace and Payson spent their early years huddled next to the wood stove in the winter and struggling to make their prized possession fly as a viable business. They envisioned the Outdoor Center as a utopian society where newcomers would be introduced to the outdoors by a group of people who passionately loved the environment and would share it with customers who would quickly become known as "guests."

The breadwinner for the center became raft guiding. Payson had been introduced to paddling as a camper and a counselor at Camp Pioneer in north Georgia, near the foot of Brasstown Bald near Helen, Georgia. He bought his first aluminum Grumman canoe in 1965 and took to paddling like the proverbial fish to water. Payson's wife Aurelia paddled the Nantahala as a camper at Merrie Woode before she met Payson and was with Payson one day in 1965, new canoe loaded on the car and ready to run the river but with no one to run it with. Campers from Camp High Rocks happened to show up and Aurelia asked them if Payson could paddle with them, which they let him do. Aurelia always credits herself with being the second woman to run the Nantahala Falls. However, I think she was the first woman to run the falls, which she did in 1954, as on the first descent of the river by my mother in 1945 the group had walked around the falls.

The first year Payson and Aurelia were the managers of the center and Horace backed them financially. They hired as many raft guides as they could find. Jimmy and Louise Holcombe—who had been raft guides on the Youghiogheny River—and David Benner—son of the author of the guidebook for North Carolina rivers, Bob Benner—were among the distinguished group that assembled at the NOC in those first years. After the first year, Payson and Aurelia became owners and Jimmy Holcombe continued as an employee, which he still is to this day.

Women were not typically thought of as raft guide material, but from the very start they could find jobs working on the river with NOC. In fact, it became apparent that women made excellent raft guides, especially trip leaders. Women tended to be much more attentive to everyone in the rafting group's overall well-being and happiness, although they could burn out just like any other raft guide.

The classic funny story is of a female raft guide who assembled her rafting guests for the typical safety talk at the put-in to the Nantahala on the peninsula that separated the old Nantahala Riverbed from the water that empties into the river coming out of the power plant. By the end of the summer, all raft guides have given this safety talk so many times they can give it in their sleep. On this day, some poor female raft guide who had had just about enough picked up a discarded Coke can and stood on a raft to give the talk. She tossed the can into the river and said, "Follow it." Supposedly, everyone jumped into their rafts and did just that. That is not typical behavior for a raft guide, but it illustrates the point that guides are human.

NOC continued to attract an impressive array of paddlers who wanted to work in a like-minded community and be on the river. Eventually thirteen NOC employees were Olympic Paddling team members, including Louise Holcombe, Russ Nichols and John Burton, who later became the president of NOC. Payson Kennedy remembers:

I think John Burton being here was important, but it really started before that. I think one of the most fortunate things was Jim Holcombe coming here our first season. Because Jim's sister Louise was on the Olympic team of '73, our second year, she came to work here and she brought her boyfriend, Russ Nicols, and they got married later, so in our second year, we had two Olympic paddlers. And then they attracted a lot of the others like Angus Morrison and Carrie Ashton and John Burton and so on. Burton being here certainly contributed, but I would say Louise and Russ being the first two actually got things going, and even before that I mentioned the Ledyard canoe club from Dartmouth coming down, so Eric Evans and those guys coming and putting down some instructional paddling helped get it going as well.

Bunny Johns remembers well those early years:

In my opinion in the late '70s and early '80s there was probably the biggest concentration of people interested in teaching paddling at the NOC—think about Ken Kastorf, Chris Spelius, Kent Ford, Carrie Ashton, I can go on and on and on. It was really a fun place because everybody was excited and they'd come back and say, guess how we taught this today. And that's how it got started. What you were talking about, the torsional rotation got started because of the shoulder dislocation. That's when people started talking about the box, keeping your arms in the box, and if you're going to brace, being in the box. Spelius brought the Olympic emphasis on the power of the torso.

Horace Holden also started the Georgia Canoe Association (GCA) at Camp Chattahoochee just before he started NOC, in response to what he saw as a need for public education. The GCA started a race on the Nantahala, which has become the oldest continuously operating race in the Southeast, the Southeasterns. In the first years of the race it consisted of a slalom race that was held at DeLebar's Rock and a downriver race on the rest of the river. The second year the slalom was moved upstream to what was then known as the First Rapid but later became known as Patton's Run, as a tribute to Charlie Patton, a one-armed paddler who was well known for his tireless enthusiasm for teaching paddling.

In 1979, Rick Bernard drowned while paddling as a safety boater on Jawbone Rapid on section four of the Chattooga for a Nantahala Outdoor Center raft trip. Rick's death sent shock waves throughout the paddling community and served as a catalyst for the development of the most comprehensive river rescue techniques the world has ever known. On that fateful trip was a guide named Slim Ray, who was later to become one of the country's most well-respected authorities and author on the subject of river rescue. Also working as a guide at the NOC at the time was a man named Les Bechdel, who was also a rock climber. Together Slim and Les wrote the book *River Rescue* and began conducting river rescue–specific clinics at NOC. I had been working as a part-time paddling instructor at NOC in the early 1980s and was invited by Les to participate in one of these clinics because of my experience as a rock climber.

My first impression was that a lot of the skills that were being practiced were not rescue techniques, but instead were body recovery techniques. In most situations, we were not carrying (and still don't on the typical one-day trip) equipment like pulleys and rock-specific anchors. Time is always an issue in any rescue situation and, in most cases, people on river trips simply don't have enough of it.

Payson Kennedy reflects,

> *I can remember when they first started teaching the rescue courses, everybody wanted to use a z-drag all the time, and a lot of the old-timers said it's a handy skill to use, and have available if you need it, but I never saw a boat I couldn't unpin more simply. That would be an exaggeration now, because I have seen one or two where we couldn't just manhandle it off, but usually, if you just look at the boat and figure which way the forces are working, you know almost always, with two or three people, get it loose and not have to set up a fancy rope system. A lot of people now just like to set up the rope system, so that's the first thing they think of.*

However, in my discussions with Ray Eaton, who was living at the time on the Nantahala, I realized that this movement was a good thing for the industry and that the preoccupation with it was going to have to run its course. I mostly kept my mouth shut and contributed whatever I could, which was a strong belief that fundamental skills like rope throwing and river swimming were anyone's first and best line of self-preservation.

Les Bechdel—NOC Chattooga outpost director, seasoned guide and National Kayak champion—had invited me to attend a river rescue staff–training weekend at the NOC. The focus of the training was to apply rock climbing techniques to the river environment. As I observed a lot of the complex "rescue" systems being used from the relative safety of the road above the Nantahala Falls where I had seen Ray sit for hours watching the display of tourist carnage, Ray shared with me some of his concerns about the river rescue movement. He felt strongly but quietly certain that any guide who got involved in using ropes in the water must have a knife. The hazard of getting tangled up in the rope was too great, even though carrying ropes is fundamentally a good idea.

I also agreed with him that a lot of these complex river rescue systems might have equipment limitations. However, Sam Fowlkes, river rescue expert, reminds me that in today's day and time, it would not be unusual for there to be a good bit of rescue equipment on the trip, especially on an oar rig trip. We definitely didn't carry any rescue equipment before 1980, except for the occasional throw rope, and we were lucky we didn't need it most of the time.

The development of river rescue as a skill was the culmination of many factors that started coming together with the writing of the Safety Code in 1957 by what was then known as the American Whitewater Affiliation, now simply American Whitewater. I remember seeing old AWA journals in the boathouse at camp, but I didn't fully appreciate the significance of the organization until years later.

Sumner Williams and Pat Stone demonstrate an early river rescue, with throw ropes, on the Nantahala River, 1960s.

Tower at Camp Mondamin waterfront, 1930s.

In looking back and talking to people, I have learned that Hugh Caldwell, the philosophy professor from Sewanee who ran the paddling program at Camp Merrie Woode, used to carry a clothesline on the river to assist with the freeing of pinned canoes. Years later, in the early 1970s, NOC started carrying half-inch-diameter polypropylene ropes and did have one with the trip the day Rick drowned.

Bob Benner began to carry and use throw ropes with Carolina Canoe Club trips in the late 1960s and early 1970s. He learned how to use the now-famous Steve Thomas Rope trick and the "Z" drag from a *Coastal Canoeist* newsletter in 1972. In 1974, Bob and Western Piedmont Community College hosted a River Rescue Symposium that was attended by Payson Kennedy, the president of the Nantahala Outdoor Center, and Charlie Walbridge, who later became the safety chairman of American Whitewater. People started carrying throw ropes around 1974 and the American Canoe Association's *Cruise Leaders Guide* contained guidelines for instructors on throwing ropes and swimming rapids. Rescue 3 was founded in 1978 in California, a river rescue–specific training school that heavily influenced Slim Ray and Les Bechdel, who later wrote the book *River Rescue*.

Rick Bernard's drowning in 1979 served as the catalyst for the development of river rescue as being just another of the many languages that river guides have to speak. In my years as a river guide I have had to free hundreds of pinned boats, mostly aluminum canoes. I usually am able to use the tethering of the pinned boat, the "ten Boy Scouts" method, to pull and maybe a log out of the woods for leverage to free the boat. My experience is mostly with canoes on easier water, but a stuck Grumman canoe can be a challenge.

While I have foreseen and prevented many near misses, I have never had to deal with a serious incident on the river. By looking ahead at most situations, most incidents can be prevented by simply saying, "What is going to happen if that kid does something out of inexperience and takes the next move in the development of a train of steps that leads to a problem?" *Not on my watch* has always been my philosophy.

LOOKING DOWNSTREAM

*And so there ain't nothing more to write about, and I am rotten glad
of it, because if I'd a knowed what a trouble it was to make a book
I wouldn't a tackled it and I ain't agoing to no more.*
—*Mark Twain,* Adventures of Huckleberry Finn, *1884*

What Are They Bitin' Today?

Homer King lived up Silver Mine Creek and built the
most beautiful wooden paddles I have ever seen. His
paddles are like fine furniture and are almost too nice
to beat up on a tortuous whitewater descent. Having
worked at NOC for years, Homer and his family were
looking for some way to stay in the gorge and remain a
part of the great community that NOC had spawned
since 1972. Crafting beautiful paddles seemed like a
good idea. Homer bought land, built a shop and opened
Silver Creek Paddles. I own a number of Silver Creek
Paddles and still prefer to use them in the winter, as the
wood grasp is warmer on the hands.

A number of years ago, with countless Nantahala runs
under his belt, Homer decided he needed to do something

Mondamin/Green Cove campers in a Grumman canoe at the
second drop of Toxaway Narrows, 1960s.

different. The Nantahala is world-renowned for excellent
trout fishing. Homer likes to fish, but paddling with the
crowds that had become emblematic had driven Homer to
consider other alternatives. He began to carry his fishing
pole on the river and found that paddling the Nantahala
was an excellent way to catch fish.

One of the issues that keeps coming up today is the
conflict between fishermen and paddlers. This seems
strange. Don't we all want the same things? Clean water,
mountain streams and access are common goals. What
would happen if paddlers started carrying fishing poles
and bought fishing licenses? Maybe they would even
discover the joy to be found in stalking a wild brown trout,
catching it on a remote section of a river that may only
be accessible by boat. As Homer King discovered, I think
there is a whole other related world out there waiting for
boaters to experience.

Paddlers are going to be most interested in boating
when the water is up. Fishermen prefer clearer, low-water

situations. Seems to me that we could establish high- and low-water levels for boating and fishing, which would please everybody. Surely this can't be that hard a conflict to resolve.

Anybody Got a Couple-a' Bucks for Gas Money?

The biggest negative that I see to paddling is our dependence on fossil fuel. Setting up a shuttle and getting everybody to the river costs the environment. As a group, paddlers tend to be environmentally minded, but they are willing to overlook this detail to support their habit.

Several years ago, I spent the summer paddling with someone who didn't like to paddle with others (go figure, since paddling is a wonderful social experience). This left us with one car, so we'd go to the river with no prearranged shuttles. We spent the whole summer paddling many rivers in Western North Carolina and never set up a two-car shuttle. I did this by going to the put-in first and dropping off my paddling partner and our equipment. I then drove to the take-out and started looking around for some help. Oftentimes I could get a ride with another boater. Many times I could hitchhike, especially on a popular river like the Nantahala. Wearing a life jacket was a good visual cue.

On the less popular rivers, especially during the week, this didn't always work. When faced with no prospects, I would look around the parking lot for a tourist. I would addle up to them, introduce myself and start some small talk about the river. Typically they loved hearing about the river from a local, and if I threw in a little history I had them.

Eventually, I'd ask, "Hey, do you think I could buy a ride from you to the put-in?"

The response was always, "No, no. We wouldn't think of charging you. Hop in."

Fritz Orr Sr. is on the right and Hugh Caldwell is in the middle; the other guy is an unknown staff member of Camp Merrie Woode.

On the way to the put-in I would continue to spin tales and give them plenty of local color and yore, not letting the facts get too much in the way of a good story. This strategy worked so well all summer that I think I cut my fuel costs in half.

Scamming shuttles and taking up fishing and is a small price to pay for boaters to enter the twenty-first century and reduce their sizable carbon footprint, and have some fun while doing it. Going online and getting valuable information, such as directions and water levels, the night before is good thinking too. How many times have you bumbled around the countryside because you didn't really know exactly how to get to the river, and it was too low when you got there anyway? I know I have done exactly that too many times. If you had a fishing license you at least could have gone fishing. Take a bike for a shuttle and you get some real exercise.

I think it's time for us, the fun-loving paddling community, to start behaving more responsibly and to account for our actions. Join American Whitewater and/or the American Canoe Association. Buy a fishing license. The boating community has gotten away with not paying for its use of our rivers for a long time. Things are changing and, despite what they say, I think you can teach an old dog a new trick. Your momma will be proud.

The River Gives Yet Another Lesson in Humility

When I was between my sophomore and junior years at Warren Wilson College, I decided to take a little time off from being a student and become a raft guide. Never mind that I had been paddling for thirteen years and had never set foot in a raft. I knew that it had to be easier than paddling a fifteen-foot Grumman down the Chattooga. I scheduled an appointment with Ray McClain, the man who was in charge of hiring at NOC, and put in a phone call to Ray Eaton to get an inside reference.

My interview seemed to go all right. During the interview I expressed the sentiment that I was unwilling to guide rafts. All I wanted to do was to teach paddling canoes, something I had been doing an excellent job of since age sixteen at camp.

Of course I didn't get the job. Ray McClain deserves credit for recognizing my youth and stupidity. In disappointment, I asked Ray Eaton what had happened. Ray told me that I had used bad judgment. I had been too demanding for an entry-level position and had embarrassed him. Now I was embarrassed. What an idiot I was.

Ray Eaton, to his credit, was understanding and pointed out my errors without being upset. He demonstrated some of that great diplomacy that he was

Camp High Rocks girls' campers in a Grumman canoe on section three, Sight on the Rock (also known as Fickle Finger Rapid or Hounds Tooth Rapid), 1964.

known for and I learned a valuable lesson. I did not work on the Nantahala that summer and I continued my education instead. I also went back to Camp High Rocks that summer and ran the paddling program for the boys' and girls' camps.

That's Why They're Called Fundamentals

Slalom racing is dying. People, especially young people, simply are not interested in slalom racing. They all want to either be play boaters or steep creekers or both. One of the challenges that faces today's play boaters is getting into the hole to perform their amazing acrobatics. Oftentimes the biggest hurdle for these people is getting from a position downstream of the hole up onto the wave itself. What most of these guys need is a strong forward stroke that would better enable them to motor around the river and go wherever they want. One of the first things you learn as a slalom paddler is how to execute a good forward stroke. Books have been written about nothing else but the forward stroke. After a lifetime of boating, I'm still working on mine. I've seen today's young boaters place ropes on trees to assist them in gaining access to a wave.

Steep creeking is all about placing your boat exactly six inches off a rock in order to take the perfectly timed boof stroke (catching an eddy using a rock to deflect off) in just the right place at just the right time. Sounds like slalom to me.

A few years ago, Chris Gragtmans became a student at Warren Wilson College. Chris is a world-renowned paddler who is sponsored and is essentially a rock star in today's paddling world. We had a whitewater racing team that had only been defeated once in the eight years I coached the program. Occasionally we would get one of these hot, young boaters at school and they consistently never had any use for our program. We didn't paddle hard enough rivers and besides, slalom was dead.

At that time, two-time Olympian, and my friend, Lecki Haller was helping me with the team. Practices on our little campus slalom course on the Swannanoa River were magical. We hung a few gates and Lecki created the most interesting and challenging courses for the students who'd show up and paddle.

Our specialty at Warren Wilson was taking a beginner who had little or no experience and turning her or him into a class-four boater in a year. We did it with slalom, as it is simply one of the optimal ways to learn "boat control." Whether a student wants to race or not, this is the best way to get better fast. To Chris's credit, he knew this, jumped in, soaked up everything he could from Lecki and in no time he rose to the top of the intercollegiate ranks.

Frank Bell in a Grumman canoe at Keyhole Rapid, on the Chattooga River, 1960s.

Increasing Water Wisdom

One of the more interesting things to do when you first encounter any river is to poke a stick in the sand at water level. Then, as the water rises or falls, you have a gauge. When running a dam-released river, watching the water rise is one of the more fascinating aspects of becoming more familiar with the river environment. Children love to watch the water come up on the stick and run around and throw rocks in the new current. I kind of like it too.

Sometimes it's fun to be running a river and be on the water just ahead of the surge from the dam. When water is released into the riverbed it must first fill each pool and then overflow into the next pool. More often, though, I've been on the river when I outran the water. That's not a good time.

Most people envision a mini tsunami washing down the river when it gets turned on. Actually, the river typically comes up to full flow in five to ten minutes at a gradual but fairly rapid pace.

Gratitude Without Attitude

To end this diatribe, I wish I could acknowledge several thousand people whom I have had the privilege of paddling with. However, every time I sit down and try to write something, the words express less than what I'm feeling. They sound trite and don't convey the depth of my emotions.

I have been blessed with a wonderful bunch of companions and students in my thirty-six-plus years of running rivers and teaching paddling. I have, with a few exceptions, been graced with their company on the river. Time and time again I have felt that they taught me as much as I teach them.

While running rapids, enduring cold water and being nearly drowned, all with multiple sclerosis, has been a serious obstacle, teaching has given me the rewards and reasons to go on. Just recently, one of my student assistants showed me a better way to explain how to shut down the inevitable flow of water up a person's nose that occurs when they turn upside down in a kayak preparing to execute an Eskimo roll. I love Emily for that tidbit as much as I love all of the people who have gone down the river of life with me. Thank you.

I think the river has taught me these and many more things. Listen to the river—its roar, splashes and gurgling. Observe the way that you and your friends interact with and respond to her sounds and moods. You may come away with a better understanding of yourself. Sometimes when scouting a rapid I feel the thud and boom of heavy water in my chest. This sound typically heightens my anxiety about running the drop. Scouting rapids becomes a mixed blessing. On one hand, you need to know what you are preparing to deal with, but the process also serves to add to your apprehension, so much so that your fear can become an impediment to the successful negotiation of the falls. It's an interesting mixed bag of psychological baggage. You have to be able to visualize yourself making the moves, but you may be terrified. Walking around a rapid is always an option. For the most part, in my years of boating, I've known rapids to change but not to disappear. If you choose to walk a drop today, chances are good that it'll be there for you to try again tomorrow.

Water is spiritual. It is the essential component of life on our planet. It needs to be respected, loved and treated as if it were the most precious thing there is, because it is. When water moves, it releases negative ions that have been proven scientifically to be soothing to the human psyche. That's one of the reasons why sleeping at the beach is so inviting. In rapids we have all kinds of moving water releasing plenty of negative ions, bathing the brain in soothing energy (no matter how freaked out you may be to run "Killer Fang Falls").

The experience of negotiating rapids can end quickly. As I've said, just like in the bedroom, you've got to slow down. Savor and enjoy the journey. Pull into an eddy and look around. Learn something about the vegetation and animals that are found in riparian zones (rivers only) and your familiar stream will come to life.

Sometimes students complain about the ease of the river chosen for the day's run. I find that a little immature and boring. Usually it's some young person, probably a guy, who would rather be off running a river that is more challenging. I smile and realize that that was me once.

Where Do I Start with These Greenhorns?

There is an ongoing debate in outdoor education, a community that uses the outdoors as a tool for personal growth: do you focus on the personal growth and development of the individual or do you teach hard skills and hope that the personal growth naturally occurs as a result of the experience? I have always been most comfortable with the approach that stresses teaching hard skills first. I think it's safer and more fun. Stopping to address someone's ignorance in missing that last eddy can be difficult. However, failure is often a better teacher than success. A good camp counselor knows when to let them burn the oatmeal.

Seeing someone who has skills and experience, and a little aptitude for structuring a field trip for students, can be an inspiring event. Sometimes I think that my reluctance to deal with interpersonal problems is a weakness on my part. However, if we are going to get down this river today, there are some things students will need to know. We can talk about Billy not helping to load the van and trailer later tonight around the campfire.

This debate about teaching techniques is widely known as the Outward Bound versus National Outdoor Leadership School (NOLS) approach. In truth, I think

Camp Mondamin campers in wooden and canvas canoes on Lake Summit, 1940s.

a little of both probably takes place. In the mid-1970s, Payson Kennedy took Karl Ronke of Outward Bound fame down a river, and out of that experience North Carolina Outward Bound started a relationship with NOC to provide whitewater instruction that was to last twenty years. As an instructor for these courses, Bunny Johns took the hands-off approach to teaching and was very successful. She would not bore the students with a lot of stroke work and river hydrodynamics. They would put in on section two of the Chattooga, a beginner run, and she would simply tell them to follow her. By the time they got to the Highway 76 bridge, the take-out for section three, three days later, the students had become efficient without lots of lecture time.

Recollections and Appreciation

I don't suppose I can finish this without saying something about history. My father was a history professor for thirty years and I was a history major in college. I have a terrible memory. While my recollection of some things is not as good as it could be, I do feel like I have an appreciation for the awareness of our past. Without looking back, we will continue to bumble around and make the same stupid mistakes over and over. We will not have an appreciation for those who have gone before us and have so generously shown the way. The stories of our forefathers of the river community are both interesting and instructive.

I am concerned that some of today's boaters, with their skateboard, surfer-dude attitudes, are missing some things. They are advancing the sport on one level, but oftentimes they do so without any understanding of the massive shoulders on which they stand. That's why I wrote this book. I hope that reading it was enjoyable for you and that you have an increased knowledge of the rich and colorful history that is part of paddling rivers in North Carolina.

Camp Mondamin campers in wooden and canvas canoes at Little Corky Rapid on the lower Green River, pre-1945.

Raymon Eaton died in 1980 and that is where my story ends. It will be a long time, maybe forever, before someone paddles with us who has the impact on the paddling community that he did. I remember when they poured his ashes in the Nantahala River just above Patton's Run. As his remains swirled into the little eddies and over the rocks, I was struck by the appropriateness of the moment. It seemed perfect. With a tear-stained face, I was overcome with the sadness and the joy of knowing that my life had been blessed by having known this extraordinary man. The fact that I am now promoting one of his key concepts—water wise—through this book, all these years after his death, warms me and makes the work involved worthwhile and important. The fact that I am maintaining his legacy as much as possible is an overwhelming emotional feeling for me. Hopefully, generations of paddlers who might never have heard of water wise will come to understand and know the concept in their own lives. At that point, my job will be done.

Frank Bell Sr.

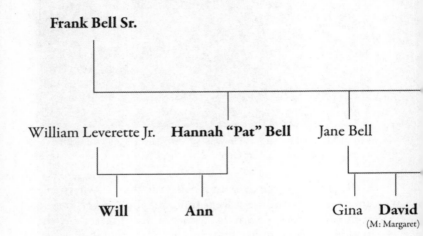

William Leverette Jr.   **Hannah "Pat" Bell**   Jane Bell

Will   **Ann**   Gina   **David**
(M: Margaret)

Frank Bell Sr. (second
marriag

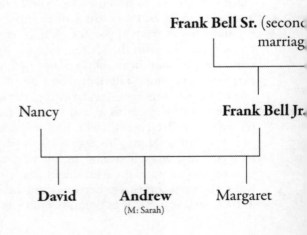

Nancy   **Frank Bell Jr.**

David   **Andrew**   Margaret
(M: Sarah)

BELL FAMILY TREE

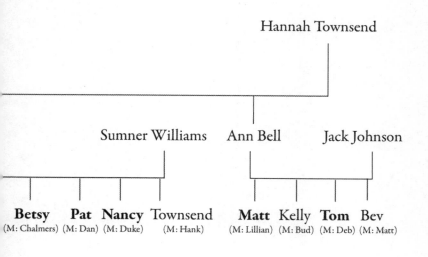

Hannah Townsend

Sumner Williams   Ann Bell   Jack Johnson

Betsy   **Pat**   **Nancy**   Townsend   **Matt**   Kelly   **Tom**   Bev
(M: Chalmers) (M: Dan) (M: Duke)   (M: Hank)   (M: Lillian) (M: Bud) (M: Deb) (M: Matt)

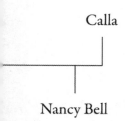

Calla

Nancy Bell

*Names in bold are paddlers

GLOSSARY

The following historical glossary contains some of the terms that we commonly used in the 1960s and '70s.

bow
the front or leading end of a boat

bump and grind
a rescue technique in which the paddler uses her boat perpendicular to the boat in trouble to push (bulldoze) the boat to shore

C-1 and C-2 (the *C* stands for canoe)
a boat that is paddled while kneeling using a single-bladed paddle; the number refers to the number of boaters

canoe paddle
consists of one blade

class one through five
American Whitewater (education-preservation organization) international scale of river difficulty grading, with class one being the easiest and class five being the hardest to descend

decked boats
fiberglass and plastic boats whose hulls are essentially enclosed and a neoprene spray skirt is worn by the boater to shed water; kayaks, C-1s and C-2s

downstream
looking down the river's current

eddy
upstream current or calm water found downstream of a rock, obstruction or on the inside of a bend

ender/pirouette
an advanced decked boat move of the 1970s, whereby a boater uses the power of a larger hydraulic or wave to perform aerial acrobatics

entrapment
getting a body part trapped or pinned by the current against a boat or other obstruction

flip
turning a boat over

Green River sandwich
pineapple and cheese, a timeless classic

gunwales
the strip of wood or aluminum that forms the upper edge of a canoe

hay-mo
standing wave

hole
depression in the river formed by falling water characterized by recirculating current found at the base of a drop

hydraulic
reverse current found in a hole

hypothermia
lowering of core body temperature due to exposure to cold water and/or wind

kayak paddle
consists of two blades

keel
strip of short, vertical boat material attached to the bottom of the boat that helps the boat to go in a straight line; the keel was used on aluminum boats to hold the two halves of the boat together

keeper
powerful hydraulic that is capable of retaining or holding a boater and/or equipment stationary

oar
used to propel rowboats; characterized by a handle

paddle
characterized by a grip on one end, used to paddle canoes and kayaks

paddling jacket
nylon shell that is used to shield the boater from splashed water or wind

painter
ropes that are attached to each end of a canoe; named for the ropes that painters used to use to attach the canoe to the side of a larger boat to be painted

PFD
personal flotation device or life jacket; Chief never owned

one, although we do have a picture of him wearing one on a cruise to Antarctica

pinned boat
a boat that is held by the current against a rock or other obstruction

put-in
the beginning of the trip

rapid
section of the river that is characterized by a loss of elevation and rocks (and fun!)

reading the river
evaluating the mechanics of each rapid's suitability for safe and fun descent from as far away as you can see back to where you are; often accomplished by scouting the river visually from the shore

ribs and planks
long strips of wood that wooden canoes are made of

river left
left side of the river relative to a person when he is facing downstream; it is still the same side even when facing upstream

river right
right side of the river relative to a person when he is facing downstream; it is still the same side even when facing upstream

scouting rapids
stopping and walking down the shore to gain a better view of the rapid

shuttle
a vehicle that drops paddlers and boats at the put-in and then picks them up again at the take-out

stern
the back or trailing end of a boat

strainer
tree or limb situated in the current that water flows through like a colander

swamp
filling a boat with water from waves or holes

take-out
the end of the trip

thwart
wood or aluminum bar that runs across a canoe from gunwale to gunwale to hold the boat together

umbrella
subsurface rock that causes the water to mound up and forms a "clamshell" on the downstream side, also known as a "pillow"

upstream
looking up the river's current

Photo by Arlin Geyer.

About the Author

Will Leverette has been an active professional member of the outdoor education/recreation community since 1972. He was the staff coordinator and program developer for a therapeutic camping program in North Carolina for juvenile delinquents for eight years. He has been an instructor trainer with the American Canoe Association for fifteen years and a whitewater river paddler for over thirty years, working as a guide and instructor in the intermountain West and the Southeast. He was a Professional Ski Instructors Association Nordic instructor and was a water safety, advanced first aid, CPR and canoeing instructor with the American Red Cross for ten years. He has worked as a risk manager and a claims consultant to the liability insurance industry since 1988 with the Worldwide Outfitter and Guide Association. Mr. Leverette now owns his own risk and crisis management consulting business, ARMOR, the Affiliation of Risk Managers for Outdoor Recreation. He assists with the whitewater paddling program at Warren Wilson College in Swannanoa, North Carolina.